# MORE SECRETS
# *of* CONSULTING

## THE CONSULTANT'S TOOL KIT

*Also Available from Dorset House Publishing*

*An Independent Publisher of Books on
Systems and Software Development and Management. Since 1984.*

- Contact us for prices, shipping options, availability, and more.
- Sign up for *DHQ: The Dorset House Quarterly* in print or PDF.
- Send e-mail to subscribe to *e-DHQ,* our e-mail newsletter.
- Visit Dorsethouse.com for excerpts, reviews, downloads, and more.

### DORSET HOUSE PUBLISHING
353 West 12th Street  New York, NY 10014  USA
1-800-DH-BOOKS  1-800-342-6657
212-620-4053  fax: 212-727-1044
info@dorsethouse.com  www.dorsethouse.com

# MORE SECRETS
## *of* CONSULTING

### THE CONSULTANT'S TOOL KIT

## GERALD M. WEINBERG

**DORSET HOUSE PUBLISHING**
**353 WEST 12TH STREET**
**NEW YORK, NEW YORK 10014**

## Library of Congress Cataloging-in-Publication Data

Weinberg, Gerald M.
    More secrets of consulting : the consultant's tool kit / Gerald M. Weinberg
        p. cm.
    Complements his The secrets of consulting (1985).
    Includes bibliographical references and index.
    ISBN 0-932633-52-8 (softcover)
        1. Business consultants. 2. Consultants. I. Title.

    HD69.C6 W448 2002
    001--dc21

                                                        2001053880

**Visit the Author on the World Wide Web: www.jerryweinberg.com**
Contact Dorset House for quantity discounts, examination copy requirements, and permissions:  Call (800) 342-6657 or (212) 620-4053 or e-mail info@dorsethouse.com. For academic permissions: Copyright Clearance Center, (978) 750-8400.

Portions of this text are adapted from the author's monthly column, "The Big Picture," in *Contract Professional,* a magazine for independent contractors and consultants.

Cover and Interior Illustrations:  Rich Terdoslavich
Cover Design:  David W. McClintock

Executive Editor:  Wendy Eakin
Senior Editor:  David W. McClintock
Editor:  Nuno Andrade
Assistant Editors:  Vincent Au, Benjamin A. Deutsch, Jessica N. Stein

Copyright © 2002 by Gerald M. Weinberg.  Published by Dorset House Publishing, 353 West 12th Street, New York, NY 10014.

Distributed in the English language in Singapore, the Philippines, and Southeast Asia by Alkem Company (S) Pte. Ltd., Singapore; in the English language in India, Bangladesh, Sri Lanka, Nepal, and Mauritius by Prism Books Pvt., Ltd., Bangalore, India.

Printed in the United States of America

Library of Congress Catalog Number:  2001053880

ISBN-10: 0-932633-52-8
ISBN-13: 978-0-932633-52-1

                        15  14  13  12  11  10  9  8  7  6  5  4  3

# Contents

# MORE SECRETS
## *of* CONSULTING

### THE CONSULTANT'S TOOL KIT

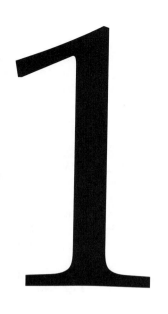

# the law of
# strawberry jam

When I mentioned to my pal Michelle that I was writing a sequel to *The Secrets of Consulting*, she shook her head in disbelief. "Why don't you quit while you're ahead? Don't you believe your own preaching? What about The Law of Raspberry Jam?"[1]

Michelle was referring to the law that describes how any Great Message gets diluted when carried too far: "The wider you spread it, the thinner it gets." She doubted that a second volume could be as good as the first.

"Yeah," she continued, "I'll grant that your first book was pretty good, so why didn't you stop when you were ahead? Are you just trying to cash in on its success?"

"Well, truthfully, Michelle, I *am* trying to cash in on the success of *Secrets*. Should I be ashamed of that?"

"Not unless you're not giving value to your readers."

"Fair enough," I said. "I'll start the book by letting the readers know what kind of value they can expect. So, let's try an analysis."

I explained to Michelle that up until now, *Secrets* has sold about 100,000 copies, and that many readers have told me how much they have increased their annual consulting income by applying such secrets as The Ten Laws of Pricing, The Orange Juice Test, Marvin's Great Secrets, The Buffalo Bridle, and The Ten Laws of Marketing. Hearing this, she mentioned that it had increased her income, too.

"By how much?" I asked.

"Oh, at least ten thousand dollars per year, and that would be conservative."

"Okay," I said, "so, assuming that each copy was read at least once, those readers have increased their earnings by one billion dollars per year in aggregate. And that's every year from now on."

"Okay," she said. "I'll buy a copy."

## THE JAM LAWS

Well, if you're like Michelle—the type who believes in numbers—that analysis ought to convince you, too. If this book is even half as good as the first, it will still be filled with enough jam to make it a delicious read.

---

[1] Gerald M. Weinberg, *The Secrets of Consulting* (New York: Dorset House Publishing, 1985), p. 11.

2

But what if you're not like Michelle? What if you need general principles to convince you? Then you'll have to read on, and learn about The Law of *Strawberry* Jam.

Young visionaries are discouraged by The Law of Raspberry Jam because they would like to believe that their message would remain thick as they spread it far and wide. But they need not be discouraged, even though no vision retains uniform thickness as it spreads. Although raspberry jam keeps getting thinner on your morning toast, any fine strawberry jam behaves quite differently.

Slather a bit of raspberry jam on a few slices of bread, and you'll see each stroke get thinner and thinner. But if you try the same trick with strawberry preserves, you'll notice that no matter how much you try to spread it, the lumps remain! Or, in the words of The Law of Strawberry Jam,

**As long as it has lumps, you can never spread it too thin.**

In strawberry jam, the lumps are strawberries. In your Great Message, the lump is you. What lumps are to strawberry jam, you are to your Great Message. As long as your medium of communication involves your own body in the flesh—speaking, writing, hugging—your message cannot be infinitely diluted. That's why I decided to write this volume about you, the individual consultant. I want to provide the personal tools you need to make your messages as lumpy as possible—certainly lumpier than those conveyed by the cloned consultants who issue forth from the big consulting factories every day.

THE LAW OF GRAPE JELLY

Ours is not an age of strawberry jam. Grape jelly seems to be the favorite covering for the American Restaurant Toast—it's absolutely without lumps or even tiny seeds. In fact, it's absolutely without taste, which eliminates complaints. You might complain that the jam tastes "off," but you can hardly complain that it has no taste whatsoever.

Not having lumps, grape jelly is perfect for processing through manufacturing machines. It's that lumpy third dimension—the depth—that makes mass production impractical. Grape jelly spreads infinitely thin, so the consumer can color a predictable number of slices of toast out of a single sterilized plastic container. With strawberry jam, there's always the danger of finding a lump, thus consuming the entire "portion control" container on a single slice of toast.

Jelly contains no surprises and it's cheaper to manufacture than jam—these two properties combine to yield The Law of Grape Jelly:

**Nobody ever bothers to complain about grape jelly.**

The Law of Grape Jelly is a law about expectations. Another way of stating this law was one of my father's favorites:

**If you don't expect much, you'll never be disappointed.**

With the sale of ideas, you can also adopt a grape jelly marketing philosophy. If you're presenting a course, it's best from the distributor's point of view to have it reduced to an outline totally lacking in lumps, so that it can be taught by any of a dozen cloned lecturers. Even better is to have it reduced to a video tape or disk that can be played anywhere and give a uniformly thin result. This approach serves to eliminate the *bad* lumps at the same time it strains out the good ones. Nobody ever found an entire caterpillar in their grape jelly. By eliminating lumpy people, you get uniform, but thin, quality.

Manufactured items are designed to be built from identical components by a series of processes that require not the slightest individuality on the part of the assemblers. Similarly, many office procedures are reduced to steps that can be carried out by anybody who can fog a mirror. Like grape jelly on white toast, the results of these processes aren't superbly satisfying, but at least they're uniform and entirely predictable. Best of all, no one complains.

THE LUMP LAW

In another book of mine, *An Introduction to General Systems Thinking,* I introduced The Lump Law:

**If we want to learn anything, we mustn't try to learn everything.**[2]

In other words, it pays to choose your lumps.

By applying The Lump Law (see, I *do* use my own principles), I convinced myself that like *The Secrets of Consulting,* this book will not attempt to cover everything a consultant ought to know. Instead, I will confine myself to a few essential tools that every consultant—and really

---

[2] Gerald M. Weinberg, *An Introduction to General Systems Thinking: Silver Anniversary Edition* (New York: Dorset House Publishing, 2001), p. 105.

everyone who ever gives or seeks advice—should always have close at hand. Hence the subtitle, *The Consultant's Tool Kit.*

Many of the other things that a consultant ought to know can be found in the books of Peter Block, who has certainly taught me a great deal. In an interview with Peter, Paula Jacobs asked: "What do you see as the single most important life lesson for consultants?" He answered as follows:

> The person is the product. Working on becoming a more authentic, whole person is the best business strategy. We are selling an intangible service, so clients have no way of knowing what they will be getting and whether they can derive value from what they get. . . . [the] more direct we are, the better human contact we make, the more centered and self aware we are, the more likely the client will see us as someone who they can lean on, someone who delivers on promises, someone they can learn from.[3]

That's exactly why I'm going to concentrate here on those tools that most help me to be direct, more centered, more self-aware, and more in contact with other people. I've derived these tools from a set that was originally given to me by the great family therapist, Virginia Satir. When she wrote the foreword to *The Secrets of Consulting,* I was just beginning to appreciate the depth of her teachings. Now, they have permeated all aspects of my life.

## SATIR'S SELF-ESTEEM TOOL KIT

Virginia, like me, was fond of metaphors and collected them from a profusion of sources, such as *The Wizard of Oz,* by Frank Baum. Remember how the Wizard gave the Scarecrow a brain, the Tin Man a heart, the Cowardly Lion a badge of courage, and Dorothy the power to go home. The Wizard's great secret was that each of them already possessed the tools they thought they lacked. The Wizard's job was merely to remind them.

From this idea, Virginia developed her idea of the "self-esteem tool kit"—a set of resources that each of us owns but often forgets to use when we're feeling powerless. As a consultant, out there alone in a sometimes unappreciative world, I've frequently reminded myself of the metaphors in Virginia's original kit:

---

[3] Paula Jacobs, interview with Peter Block, *CPUniverse Newsletter* (Oct. 27, 2000).

The Wisdom Box—the ability to know what's right and what's not right for me. Without a Wisdom Box, I would find myself forever working in situations that violated my principles, or for which I had no energy.

The Golden Key—the ability to open up new areas for learning and practicing, and to close them if they don't fit for me at this time. Without this Golden Key, my consulting would become narrowly focused, or focused on areas in which I was no longer interested.

The Courage Stick—the courage to try new things and to risk failure. Without my Courage Stick, my consulting turns to grape jelly.

The Wishing Wand—the ability to ask for what I want, and if necessary, to live with not getting it. Without the ability to ask for what I want, I am powerless to be an effective negotiator.

The Detective Hat, sometimes teamed with The Magnifying Glass—the ability to examine data and to reason about those data. Without analytical abilities, I would become a *solution-problemer*—a vendor of off-the-shelf, portion-controlled solutions—rather than a problem-solver responding to my clients' real needs.

The Yes/No Medallion—the ability to say yes, the ability to say no (thank you), and the ability to mean what I say. Without a yes that means yes and a no that means no, I would pander to my clients' prejudices and my advice would be worthless.

These six tools formed Virginia's self-esteem tool kit, as I learned it. Over the years, however, various colleagues have helped me add other tools to my personal version of the kit:

The Heart—the ability and willingness to put my heart into my work. My colleague Jean McLendon introduced The Heart to my kit; she explained that Virginia left it out of her kit because she assumed people always have access to their heart. Working in technical environments, though, I've learned that I often need to be reminded of the hopes and wishes and fears and sensitivities of others. The Heart gives me that nudge when I need it.

The Mirror—the ability to see *myself* and to seek and use feedback. I'd always known that feedback was important for personal growth, but I learned much more about it as I worked with Edie and Charlie Seashore on our book about feedback, *What Did You Say?*[4] Feedback is the mirror by which I can see myself and monitor how I am affecting those around me—but it only works if I remember to look in that mirror that others offer.

The Telescope—the ability to see *others* and to bring them closer to my understanding than my naked eye and brain can manage. My Telescope partners with my Mirror, which reminds me to see myself.

The Fish-Eye Lens—the ability to see the *context*, what surrounds me and others and influences us as we work together. It reminds me to *use* the many observational and analytical tools I already have, many of which I've written about in my books yet fail to recall when I most need them. Together, The Mirror, The Telescope, and The

Fish-Eye Lens equip me with the self, other, and context from Virginia's model of congruence—the ingredients that must be balanced if I am to be congruent.

---

[4] C. Seashore, E. Seashore, and G.M. Weinberg, *What Did You Say? The Art of Giving and Receiving Feedback* (North Attleboro, Mass.: Douglas Charles Press, 1992).

The Gyroscope—the ability to be balanced, to use *all* of my tools, and to be congruent or centered. My father gave me my first gyroscope, and to this day, I remain fascinated by its ability to restore its balance when disturbed. Sometimes, I think that The Gyroscope is too complex a tool for my kit, but then I remember that restoring balance to my life *is* complex and that it is something I must always try to do.

The Egg—the ability to grow, develop, and learn, using all the parts of myself that I need. Although I like to collect eggs—beautiful stone ones, usually—I'm allergic to the chicken kind. Perhaps this allergy explains why I took so long to associate The Egg with Virginia Satir's Seed Model—the concept that each of us comes into the world  with all the tools we need to be complete human beings. When I'm stuck, my Egg reminds me of the many tools I don't realize I have—and of my ability to choose or create my own tools.

The Carabiner—the ability to ensure my safety and to not take unnecessary risks—so I *can* take risks when necessary. For those of you not familiar with mountain climbing, the carabiner is a metal loop used to attach climbing ropes to pitons—hooks embedded in a cliff face. They are meant to prevent climbers from the dangers of falling. Linda Swirczek, who was an avid climber, gave me The Carabiner for my self-esteem tool kit. The Carabiner gives me that moment to double-check my actions, so I can move ahead with the confidence the situation requires.

The Feather—the ability to tickle myself and others, and not to take things, or myself, too seriously. I learned about tickling from my father, Harry Weinberg, though it was a long time before I learned much about the right timing for tickles. The Feather reminds me that, as Oscar Wilde said, "Life is too important to be taken seriously."

The Hourglass—the ability to make time for the good and to make good use of time. For me, The Hourglass is one of my most important tools because it's one that I tend to forget.

The Oxygen Mask—the symbol for a balanced life. It reminds me of my ability to breathe, which symbolizes my need to take care of myself before attempting to help others. My colleague Eileen Strider added The Oxygen Mask to my kit, reminding me of the safety instructions given on planes: "Before helping others with their oxygen mask, be sure your own mask is securely in place and operating properly." My Oxygen Mask reminds me to operate from a healthy place, the place from which I'm most likely to be able to help others, rather than inflict help that may prove harmful should I crash and burn and fail to follow through. The Oxygen Mask reminds me to use all of my other tools and to keep myself healthy and sane.

So, that's my tool kit as it stands today, and it serves me well in my roles as consultant, friend, husband, father, grandfather, and most of all, human being. I hope you'll join me in the following chapters as I show you how I use these tools. I know my kit isn't complete, though, and perhaps someday you will help me add the tools that you've found useful in your consultant's tool kit.

## *the wisdom box*

We don't receive wisdom; we must discover it for ourselves
after a journey that no one can take for us or spare us.
—Marcel Proust

Having chosen the consultant's tool kit as the organizing theme of this book, I was immediately faced with the problem of which tool should be presented first. Since the tools form a system, there can be no right answer to the question of which is first, so I decided to go by my own personal preference, The Wisdom Box.

The Wisdom Box represents my ability to know what's right and what's not right for me. Without a Wisdom Box, I would find myself forever working in situations that violated my principles, or for which I had no energy.

Although The Wisdom Box is the first tool I discuss in this book, it certainly wasn't the first I acquired, and it wasn't acquired in one chunk. Like most people, I've acquired what little wisdom I have one tiny piece at a time.

## REDDING'S READING RULE

I first learned about the importance of wisdom from a schoolmate in college, Mr. Redding. I refer to him as *Mr.* Redding because I can no longer remember his first name and because Professor Freeble always called on his students using their family names, always stressing their titles—*Miss* Warfield, *Mr.* Campbell, *Mrs.* Stein, and of course, *Mr.* Redding. Freeble was a straight-laced English professor for whom, fifty-odd years ago, I graded freshman papers.

Freeble had his favorites, and in my estimation, some of them didn't deserve his high esteem. So, each grading period, Freeble would "demonstrate" his reasons for granting his protégés higher grades than I had meted out. At these correctional meetings, Freeble usually took the opportunity to grade down some of my "inflated" grades—and *Mr.* Redding invariably suffered.

My estimation of Redding's work always exceeded Freeble's. I remember most clearly one occasion on which Redding had written a brilliant essay, but one that wasn't based on the reading Freeble had assigned. Freeble downgraded him—failed him, in fact. That left me the task of explaining to Redding why his brilliance wasn't going to be rewarded if he didn't follow the assignments.

"Too bad," Redding replied, indifferently.

"What's too bad?"

"Oh, I can't waste my time reading Freeble's assignments. Life's too short. I never read *anything* that isn't *worth* reading."

And there it was, Redding's Reading Rule:

**Never read anything that isn't worth reading.**

By happenstance, that same semester I was taking a speed-reading course in one of the World War II Quonset huts still gracing the University of Nebraska campus. Speed reading was the sort of low-status subject that didn't merit a brick-and-mortar building—let alone Grecian columns or actual college credit—but I figured that even a small increase in my reading speed would prove worth the investment of time and energy.

Three lessons into the course, I had managed to increase my speed by about 200 words per minute. I was quite proud of my accomplishment—until Mr. Redding rudely deflated me with his rule. What good is 200 words per minute when simply by *not reading* what isn't worth reading, I can instantly triple or quadruple my speed?

Redding's Rule made such an impression on me that I eagerly applied it to other activities in my crowded, four-major college curriculum. I believe I gained a substantial advantage over my less enlightened fellow students, but somehow the advantage wasn't what it should have been. More than a decade passed before I discovered why, thanks to a principle I call Cary's Crap Caution.

CARY'S CRAP CAUTION

After leaving the hallowed halls of academe, I began my career in computing and subsequently my career in writing about computing. After publishing a few technical books of my own, I was invited to resume the job of critic I had abandoned to Professor Freeble. My editor-in-chief, Cary Baker, provided a stream of technical manuscripts and checks, for which I provided a return stream of opinions on how these manuscripts could be improved.

After three of these manuscripts had been published—incorporating many of my suggestions and corrections—I had once again grown inflated with my own accomplishments.

Cary's fourth manuscript, however, was beyond the range of even my enlightened redemption. In the first place, the author didn't know anything about the subject; in the second, he didn't know much about the English language. In fact, the manuscript was so bad that it was good—good, that is, for the sadistic delight of shredding it into tiny editorial pieces.

I was living in Greenwich Village at the time, so I hand-carried my critique, all forty-two pages of it, uptown to the jade green McGraw-Hill tower. I was eager to receive Cary's praises face-to-face.

But no praise was forthcoming. Instead, Cary merely weighed the neatly typed critique in his left hand and asked, "What's all this?"

"It's my comments on the manuscript," I said proudly.

He glanced at the last page. *"Forty-two* pages? On *that* manuscript?"

"I wanted to be thorough."

"Oh, and do you gift wrap your garbage? This one wasn't worth more than two sentences."

And so, at long last, I learned that Redding's Reading Rule could be generalized to just about anything. I called this generalization Cary's Crap Caution:

**Anything not worth doing is not worth doing right.**

Or, in Cary's more vernacular form,

**Never gift wrap garbage.**

That was the first time I consciously realized that I possessed a Wisdom Box, though at the time, I didn't know what to call it. The name was to come many years later, when I met Virginia Satir.

My Wisdom Box is a first-order guide to what I ought to be doing—and especially what I ought *not* to be doing. Before learning Cary's Crap Caution, my first-order guides were different. Sometimes, I grabbed the task that paid the most money. More often, I was snared by the intriguing nature of some problem to be solved, or by the pitiful pleadings of some poor soul in need. And once I began a task, I was easily trapped by my perfectionism into doing a superb job of polishing crap that never should have been produced in the first place.

Looking back on my life as a problem-solver, I now realize that I've always had a Wisdom Box, but wasn't terribly conscious or consistent in using it. For instance, my conversation with Mr. Redding wasn't the end of the story of Professor Freeble.

FREEBLE'S FEELING FILTER

The fifth time Professor Freeble overrode my grades to reward the guilty
and punish the innocent, I finally heard that tiny internal voice say,
"Enough!"

The voice was so compelling that at first I actually thought Freeble
had said something. But it wasn't his reedy voice. Some part of me
knew that something was terribly *wrong* with Freeble's flimsy excuses
for altering grades. Though I didn't recognize it at the time, that part of
me was my Wisdom Box.

When my Wisdom Box speaks, I *know* it speaks the truth. For one
thing, there's that compelling voice, which isn't like any of my other
internal voices. So, even though I was earning the magnificent sum of
ninety cents an hour for reading Freeble's papers, when that voice
spoke, I handed him his gradebook and resigned. I also said a few
things that weren't so wise—but my Wisdom Box was still immature.

Immature though it was, my sense of what was right and what was
wrong made me realize the following:

> **Anything I shouldn't be doing, I shouldn't be doing.
> Period.**

I call this Freeble's Feeling Filter, and it applies equally to things that
aren't worth doing and things that, though worth doing by *somebody*, are
wrong for *me*. I've memorialized Professor Freeble to remind me of the
feeble excuses I concoct when I'm trying to ignore my Wisdom Box.

IS IT WISDOM OR IS IT MEMORY?

Although I was born fully equipped with a Wisdom Box, I needed substantial practice before I learned to use it well. For one thing, a Wisdom
Box speaks in various ways. In Freeble's office, it used words to put me
on alert. Sometimes, it sings to me; I wrote about my Songmeister in *The
Secrets of Consulting*.[1] Mostly, though, my Wisdom Box communicates
through a general feeling that permeates my body, a feeling I can interpret as wrong or right. Although this feeling doesn't come through my
nose, if I had to choose a sense, I'd say it's a *smell*.

Virginia Satir herself often used a *taste* metaphor. "Take a bite,"
she'd say about some new idea, "and see how it tastes. If it's good,
swallow it, but if it doesn't fit for you, spit it out." But if the new situation resembles an earlier one, it's not always easy to take that one bite.

---

[1] Gerald M. Weinberg, *The Secrets of Consulting* (New York: Dorset House Publishing, 1985), pp. 101–3.

Your Wisdom Box seems to be saying, "Don't bite on *that!* That's just like the time you . . ." As you grow older, you have more memories of mistakes and more chances to mistake one of these memories for wisdom. If all your Wisdom Box does is accumulate old lessons that prevent you from doing things, soon you'll be doing nothing at all. True, you'll never do anything *wrong*—but is that what you really want?

When you first get the old feeling, ask yourself: Have I already gone beyond this? (In other words, Is this the feeling, or a memory of the feeling?) The voice tells you whether this is here-and-now wisdom, or there-and-then.

## WISDOM BOX MISTAKES

Mistaking the past for the present is only one of several common mistakes that you can make with your Wisdom Box. Here are some others.

You can't transplant a Wisdom Box from one person to another. This is *your* Wisdom Box, not your morality bible. It won't work for other people. If you must offer wisdom from your collection, be prepared for rejection—that may be the other person's Wisdom Box doing its job.

The reverse is also true. Don't expect that you can simply transfer wisdom from another person's Wisdom Box by reading, listening to, or memorizing "words of wisdom." Wisdom comes from experience, perhaps seasoned with words, but only seasoned. Remember, you can't live on a diet of salt.

Because each Wisdom Box is personal, it is not an aid in judging others. For goodness' sake, don't be righteous about when you think others are acting unwisely. Being righteous helps even less than being right.

Now that I've warned you about transplantation, I'm certainly not so stupid as to shower you with the contents of my Wisdom Box. Besides, if you've read some of my other books, you've probably had your fill of what passes for wisdom in my mind.

Nevertheless, there are some special gems in my Wisdom Box that I'd like to offer for you to taste. These gems are not simply wisdom, but wisdom-about-wisdom, or meta-wisdom. I offer them because you'll want to be sure that your own Box has a few such meta-gems to keep it functioning properly.

*Limit Your Rationality*

A good example of meta-wisdom in action is the way I just ignored my own advice about sharing the contents of my Wisdom Box. In doing so, I applied The Rule of Restrained Rationality:

**Don't be rational; be reasonable.**

Why? I can think of several reasonable reasons:

- I am human, and no human can be completely rational all the time. If I attempt to be so, I will merely appear more foolish than people normally do.

- Since you're reading this book, I can assume that you expect certain reasonable things from me as the author—like some examples of what I consider wisdom.

- Rationality depends on tight chains of reasoning, so one weak link can break a chain of rationality. Reasonableness uses multiple chains to arrive at conclusions— some rational, some emotional; some data-based, some intuitive; some internally derived, some from external sources. Thus, reasonableness may not be as sharp and efficient, but it's more secure and less likely to lead to monstrous mistakes.

- Nobody likes a wiseass.

*Beware of Rationalizations*

Another reason for me to be reasonable is that some of the wisdom in my Box isn't very wise at all. Here, the meta-wisdom says,

**Not everything that sounds wise is wise.**

Some of the truisms in my Box are merely rationalizations that pass for rationality. This preposterous junk must be expunged and relegated to my Witless Box—the place I keep the memories of all the silliness I once believed was wisdom. I received most of this foolishness as a youth. One of the false gems in my Witless Box is the rationalization my mother gave me for the way a cut or abrasion burned when she swabbed anti-septic over it:

**If it hurts, it must be good for you.**

I call this common misbelief The Antiseptic Absurdity, and it's on a par with that sign you see in restaurants:

**Good food takes time.**

Sure, *some* things that hurt are good for you, and *some* good food takes time to prepare. But, as enunciated, both of these fallacies are rationali-zations for poor service. I put this observation in my Wisdom Box in terms of consulting:

**If they tell you it *must* be good for you because it hurts, get yourself a different consultant.**

This is one of many maxims in my Wisdom Box about when to get rid of consultants.

## Eschew False Reasoning

Sometimes, I misapply the wisdom in my Box through false reasoning—inverse implications are common examples:

- Although good food may take time, slow food can still be bad.

- Even if hurting demonstrated that the treatment is good for you, there may be good treatments that don't hurt at all.

Let me illustrate misapplied wisdom with the story of my Mercenary Maxim, which has to do with making money, and failing to make money.

In my entire consulting career, there have been only two clients who swindled me out of money that I earned. In both cases, they were promoters who put on conferences for the sole purpose of making money.

I have, at times, fallen victim to this mentality myself. Early in my writing career, I allowed an editor to persuade me that a textbook written by me would surely be a best-seller. I didn't believe in textbooks—and I still don't—but I wrote that one. To this day, that textbook is the only one of my books to flop financially.

From these and other examples, I've acquired the following wisdom, what I call The Mercenary Maxim:

> **One of the best ways to lose lots of money is to do something only for the money.**

However, at a certain period of my life, I mistakenly adhered to an inversion of this maxim:

> **One of the best ways to make lots of money is to do something without regard for the money.**

Alas, although I've had an occasional windfall while working without regard for money, this reasoning failed to be consistently true. To make a living as a consultant, I have to think about money when I negotiate contracts. It turned out that the wisdom was in not thinking *only* about the money:

> **If you want to make a living as a consultant, think about money but watch out for other important things.**

What important things? Number one on the list would be the character of the people you're dealing with—as in, "Are they thinking only about the money?"

> **Mistrust greed, especially your own.**

### Know Your Limits

Wisdom often takes the form of knowing the limits of your knowledge. My Wisdom Box knows that I don't know everything, but in some situations, I allow myself to be overcome with the feeling of absolute mastery. Every time I succumb to this temptation, I make a fool of myself.

All swindlers—including the promoters who swindled me—understand this meta-wisdom principle, which I call The Sucker Syndrome:

> **It's easiest to fool the people who know everything.**

CHECK YOUR WISDOM BOX PERIODICALLY

As I've grown older, I've grown more forgetful.  I think somebody
warned me about that, but I forget who it was.  I do remember, though,
that the person told me to make lists so I wouldn't forget important
tasks.  This seemed like a good idea, but then I always forgot to look at
the lists.

To conclude this chapter, I was planning to give you a list of all the
possible ways to misuse a Wisdom Box.  You can guess what happened
to that list.  But that doesn't matter, because I've learned that if something is really important, I'll remember it when it comes time to write
about it.  In this case, the most important thing I know about my
Wisdom Box is that I frequently forget to consult it in time, just as I do
with my lists.

Real life isn't like writing—you seldom have the luxury to wait for
your Wisdom Box to catch up with real-time events.  And remember The
Main Maxim:

> **What you don't know may not hurt you, but what you
> don't remember always does.**[2]

This is especially true when you don't remember your Wisdom Box.  For
instance, people often realize that they're in a bad situation—a job, an
assignment, a marriage—but somehow persist for years without turning
on their Wisdom Box.  For example, I've known some women who have
divorced abusive husbands, and from what they've told me, it took each
of them about three years to hear what their Wisdom Box was saying.
With abusive bosses, or clients, there seems to be a similar time span.
So, where is The Wisdom Box during all this time?

I suspect that it creeps up, the way fat creeps around my waist one
pastry at a time—a particularly insidious version of The Fast-Food Fallacy:

> **No difference plus no difference plus no difference plus
> . . . eventually equals a clear difference.**[3]

Here's the meta-wisdom from my Box: Some Wisdom Boxes have built-
in alarm clocks—warnings that flash as the situation gets dangerous.
But some Boxes also have snooze buttons that allow us to ignore these
warnings, no matter how loud they are.

---

[2] *The Secrets of Consulting,* p. 92.
[3] *The Secrets of Consulting,* p. 131.

When you're in a situation that changes by sneaks and slithers, it's safest to have built-in checkpoints that will force you to check your Wisdom Box periodically. For instance,

- I never make long-term contracts with my clients. That way, we have to renegotiate our situation at reasonable intervals, and these negotiations give me time to decide whether or not the arrangement is still wise for me.

- In the shorter term, I like to take long walks in nature. I find the natural world to be awash with wisdom of its own, wisdom that primes my own Wisdom Box.

- Long walks can be a kind of meditation, but if that's not convenient, I take short meditations wherever I happen to find myself—in airports, standing in queues, waiting for Internet access. Even the shortest meditation can rouse my Wisdom Box from its dangerous slumber.

- I especially like to take long car trips through the mountains with my wife and partner, Dani. With no distractions but the natural sights of the trip, I can tap into Dani's wisdom and my own—and take the time to remember my wisdom and to decide what of hers fits for me.

Now that you've seen my list, I ask, What wisdom checkpoints have you built into your life?

## 3

## *the golden key*

One's first step in wisdom is to question everything—and
one's last is to come to terms with everything.
—Georg Christoph Lichtenberg

$\mathbf{M}$y Golden Key is a close companion to my Wisdom Box, because I cannot acquire wisdom without the risk of traveling to unexplored realms. The Golden Key represents my ability to open new areas for learning and practicing, and also to close them when they don't fit for me at this time. Without my Key, my consulting would become narrowly focused, or focused on areas in which I was no longer interested.

## NOSY BUT NICE

I've always had a fully functional Golden Key. Perhaps I was given this Key by my father, who instead of pretending to have an answer for every question always asked me in return, "How can we find that out?" or "Where can we go to get that information?" Sometimes, we explored things together. If he did offer an answer, he never just popped it out, whole. Instead, he always unraveled his chain of mental exploration for my inspection.

Like my father, I'm a nosy guy—and I don't just mean the prominent proboscis I inherited from him. I investigate things I don't understand and stop when I'm no longer learning. Probably, that's why I've written so many books. Researching a book is my standard excuse for exploring, prying, or snooping.

Many of my books started with a question—the best ones always did. Some actually have questions for titles: *Are Your Lights On?* and *What Did You Say?*[1]

Others had questions behind them, Golden Keys that opened doors for my mind:

- My doctoral research, "Experiments in Problem Solving," asked, "Where do 'aha' experiences come from?"[2]

---

[1] Donald C. Gause and Gerald M. Weinberg, *Are Your Lights On? How to Figure Out What the Problem Really Is* (New York: Dorset House Publishing, 1990), and C. Seashore, E. Seashore, and G.M. Weinberg, *What Did You Say? The Art of Giving and Receiving Feedback* (North Attleboro, Mass.: Douglas Charles Press, 1992).

[2] Gerald M. Weinberg, "Experiments in Problem Solving," Ph.D. Thesis, University of Michigan, 1965.

- *An Introduction to General Systems Thinking* asked, "What are the general laws of thought that apply to virtually every complex situation?[3]

- *The Psychology of Computer Programming* posed the query, "What are the mental and emotional processes underlying the act of programming computers?"[4]

- When Don Gause and I wrote *Exploring Requirements,* we wanted to know, "How do we find out what people *really* want?"[5]

- The four volumes of my *Quality Software Management* series are all based on the question, "How do managers affect the quality of software produced under their stewardship?"[6]

In fact, this book, itself, started with the question, "What are the most powerful tools that all successful consultants need?"

## POLANSKI'S POINTER

Well, writing's not for everyone, but there are many other ways to activate your Golden Key.

For example, after I had learned something about programming computers, I was often asked to help people find errors in their programs. At first, I didn't have much wisdom about debugging, as this activity is sometimes called, and I wasted a lot of time following false clues.

Finally, one rainy December morning in the District of Columbia, my eyes were opened. My team was working to a hard deadline—a scheduled rocket launch—and one of the programs just wouldn't run properly. Wally, one of the programmers, called on me for help, saying that he and some other programmers had worked all night without locating the problem. I asked him what they had already figured out.

---

[3] Gerald M. Weinberg, *An Introduction to General Systems Thinking: Silver Anniversary Edition* (New York: Dorset House Publishing, 2001).

[4] Gerald M. Weinberg, *The Psychology of Computer Programming: Silver Anniversary Edition* (New York: Dorset House Publishing, 1998).

[5] Donald C. Gause and Gerald M. Weinberg, *Exploring Requirements: Quality Before Design* (New York: Dorset House Publishing, 1989).

[6] Gerald M. Weinberg, *Quality Software Management, Vols. 1–4* (New York: Dorset House Publishing, 1992–1997).

"One thing I'm absolutely sure of," Wally said, "is that the bug can't be in the Red program. I've checked that one six times. And Sarah checked it, too."

So, taking him at his word, I plunged right into the Blue, Green, and Yellow programs and never came out. That is, I didn't come out for lunch, and I didn't come out for dinner—both significant events in my working day. Finally, at around 9:30 that night, my stomach told me that Polanski's Deli, next door, was going to close in half an hour. So, I took a break.

When I got there, Polanski's crew had already cleaned up for closing, so I asked Julie, the counter waitress, for a take-out of corned beef—extra lean.

"All our corned beef is extra lean," Julie insisted while assembling the sandwich. She turned and called out, "Hey, Polanski, bring me one of those take-out bags."

"Harold must have put 'em away," Polanski shouted from the back. "Do you know where he put them?"

"No, but I'm sure they're not in the cookie cabinet. I already looked in there."

"Thanks," Polanski shouted back, and in a moment, he emerged from the kitchen, proudly displaying a brown paper bag.

"Where'd you find it?" Julie asked. "I can never find stuff that Harold puts away."

"They were in the cookie cabinet."

I was dumbfounded. "But why did you look there?" I asked. "Julie just told you she was sure they weren't there."

"Precisely," said Polanski. "When Julie's *that* sure it's not there, it means that she *believes* it's not there, so she probably never looked there. So, it's probably there."

"Oh," I muttered. I grabbed my sandwich, paid the check, and rushed back to the office.

When I arrived, Wally was still studying the errant code. "Give me the Red listing," I insisted.

"Why?" Wally questioned, but handed me the listing anyway. "We know it's not there."

"Precisely," I said, and proceeded to find the bug in about two minutes.

And that's how I learned another way to use my Golden Key, a technique I call Polanski's Pointer:

**If they're *absolutely sure* it's not there, it's probably there.**

Polanski's Pointer tells me what doors to open, and a corollary tells me which ones to leave shut:

**Don't bother looking where everyone is pointing.**

After all, if people knew the right place to look, they wouldn't ask a consultant to help them find it.

And there's another version of Polanski's Pointer, one that I apply when I find myself pointing away from some subject.

**Whenever you believe that a subject has nothing for you, it probably has something for you.**

Why? Well, if it's a subject, *somebody* is interested in it, so there's definitely something about it capable of arousing human interest. Therefore, if I don't see anything interesting about it, I must not even know enough about it to know how it can be interesting. It's a sure sign that I'll learn something when I open that closed door.

## THE GOLDEN LOCK

I have a trick for applying this personal version of Polanski's Pointer. I search for someone who is genuinely interested in the subject, and then I ask them for the one reference they would recommend to someone who knows nothing about the subject. This always works—unless I find someone who doesn't really love the subject but is just making a living at it. There's a difference.

The reason there's a difference is that most people don't make full use of their Golden Key, and thus they easily get stuck in a field that bores them. I call this phenomenon The Golden Lock:

**I'd like to learn something new, but what I already know pays too well.**

The Golden Lock is a close cousin to The Golden Handcuffs, which corporations use to shackle their most valuable employees. But unlike the Handcuffs, the Lock is self-imposed, self-designed. Being self-designed, it's a far better trap than any Handcuffs could ever be, and only The Golden Key can unlock it.

The pay for wearing The Golden Lock need not be money, though that's surely common among consultants. Quite frequently, the pay is prestige, or the envy of one's colleagues, or the gratitude of one's clients. Whatever the pay, it's not easily dispensed with—and thus the Lock.

That's why The Golden Key has two aspects—one that opens doors, and one that locks them again. I like to think my Golden Key is also very good at locking doors, but compared to Dani, I'm a novice. Dani is particularly good at locking doors and moving on, having mastered and practiced in several different areas of human knowledge: teaching piano, teaching and applying anthropology, consulting to large organizations, and training professional dog trainers.

Over the years, I believe I've learned Dani's secret rule, which I call Dani's Decider:

**When you stop learning new things, it's time to move on.**

Dani's Decider is one of the most powerful secrets of consulting. Why? Consultants are hired for knowing what others don't know, so a consultant who stops learning soon decays in value. On the other hand, the less you know, the less likely you are to threaten your clients with change, and this could endear you to those who benefit from the status quo. However, Dani's Decider would still apply, and ultimately, your value as a consultant would be diminished.

## LOCK LANGUAGE

We know that consultants can be threatening to their clients, especially if they're adept with their Golden Keys. That's why we often find our clients using lock language to keep us from opening their closets and seeing their real or imagined skeletons.

Some lock language is very direct. I've had clients invite me to examine their organizations and then tell me up front, "These are the things we don't want you to look at."

Sometimes, when I apply Polanski's Pointer and say I want to look into X, my client says, "No, I *forbid* you to look at X."

"Forbid" is rather direct lock language, but those with less authority tend to be more subtle. Possibly the most common lock phrase I hear is, "They won't like it if you ask about X."

Naturally, it's never very clear who "they" are, so I always counter with, "Oh, I didn't know that. Can you tell me who 'they' are, so I can go ask their permission?" Generally, the speaker can't or won't identify a specific person, but if they do, I simply go to that person and ask about X.

An even more subtle way of locking doors is built into us by years of schooling—schooling that teaches many of us not to ask too many questions. Certainly, I can understand why a teacher burdened with a large class of obstreperous children would want to restrict the number of questions per student, but these conditions don't apply to obstreperous consultants. So, when clients show nonverbal signs of impatience with my questions, I simply inquire, "Am I asking too many things at once? I can come back if this is too much for now."

Of course, part of what makes my Golden Key golden is my skill at getting information that's behind locked doors—and getting it without provoking locking reactions in my clients. If I've done a good job of entering the client's system, I'm not likely to trigger any forbidding. Or, at least, I've avoided making contracts with clients whose locks are going to make it impossible for me to do what they're paying me for.

I've also learned not to ask endless streams of questions. I don't need to, because I have so many other ways of getting information, as I've described in several of my books.[7] So, I don't get much hard, direct forbidding, but if I'm not careful, my clients can lull my Golden Key to sleep with an evasive lullaby.

## LULLABY LANGUAGE

Late one summer, I was called in to help an IT client learn to work better with its customers. I don't ordinarily travel in the summer, but this sounded like a real emergency, one in which I had to be on the scene to calm down both parties. The customers were enraged with the IT manager because a new system wasn't ready on time, and the IT manager was enraged with the customers because they hadn't delivered some essential information as promised, thus causing the entire project to lag its schedule by four months.

When I arrived, the temperature outside had crossed 100 degrees— but it was even hotter inside my client's conference room, emotionally. Jeff, the IT manager, smacked the table and said, "You *promised* that the component pricing data would be in our hands by February first."

Penny, the catalog manager, gave him a steely-eyed glare and muttered, "We never promised that. Never!"

"Yes, you did!"

"No, we didn't."

---

[7] See, for example: *The Secrets of Consulting* (New York: Dorset House Publishing, 1985); *What Did You Say?* with Charles and Edie Seashore (North Attleboro, Mass.: Douglas Charles Press, 1992); *Exploring Requirements,* with Donald C. Gause (New York: Dorset House Publishing, 1989); *Rethinking Systems Analysis & Design* (New York: Dorset House Publishing, 1988); and *Quality Software Management, Vol. 2: First-Order Measurement* (New York: Dorset House Publishing, 1993).

And then they looped back to the beginning of their argument, as they had several times already, raising the temperature a few degrees.

I thought that the problem solving would go better if I could cool things down, but all I was hearing was "yes-you-did-no-we-didn't," back and forth. I decided to attempt to establish some facts that were not a matter of opinion, so I asked for the original requirements document. Both Penny and Jeff seemed a bit stunned by this reference to data, but then Penny recovered and said, "Yes, that will *prove* my point."

"No, it will prove *my* point," Jeff countered. "Good idea, Jerry. Now we'll see whose fault this is."

I was a bit surprised at how readily they each found the document. (Many of my clients seem to lose the requirements documents once a project is under way.) Jeff got his open first, and placed his index finger on the following key line:

> The Catalog Department should deliver component pricing data by 1 February to the IT Department.

I assumed Penny would find some other statement to prove her point, but a few moments later, she had her copy open to the same page, upon which the same sentence was highlighted in neon pink.

"There," she said, triumphantly. "There's my proof. We *never* promised to deliver that data that early."

"Yes, you did," Jeff said. "It's perfectly clear, right there. *Should* deliver by 1 February."

"Exactly," Penny countered. "It doesn't say we *will*, but only that we *should*. And we did try. But you computer people apparently don't appreciate the difficulty of getting every single one of those prices signed off by every person involved."

After this, I eventually got things cooled down. We moved from blaming to problem solving, but not before I extracted a promise from both parties to attend a little workshop I designed for them. I designed the workshop because I didn't want to have to come back the next summer when they ran into the same problem—a lack of understanding of the ambiguity of the English language. Following are some excerpts from that workshop:

*Should*

I started the workshop by focusing on their original problem, the nasty little word, "should." Jeff read the original statement as,

The Catalog Department [must] deliver component pricing data by 1 February to the IT Department.

Penny, however, interpreted the "should" differently, as,

The Catalog Department [will make every effort to] deliver component pricing data by 1 February to the IT Department.

What I suggested was a safer meaning:

The Catalog Department [probably won't] deliver component pricing data by 1 February to the IT Department.

"Oh," said Jeff, "if I'd realized that, we could have designed the project differently. Could Catalog have delivered parts of the pricing data by February first?"

"Sure," said Penny. "We actually had about ninety percent of it by then, but that last ten percent—mostly new items—took all the work."

"Ah. If only we'd known. We didn't need the entire table to proceed. Next time, we'll just let you know what we really need."

Jeff had given me the perfect opening for the next lesson.

## Just

"Sorry, Jeff," I said. "That won't do."

"Why not?"

"Because you've managed to sneak in another one of those discounting words."

"Which word?"

"Just." I went to the whiteboard and wrote what he said:

Next time, we'll just let you know what we really need.

"Now, what's the difference between that sentence and this one?" I wrote,

Next time, we'll let you know what we really need.

"Well, it's the same thing, isn't it?"

Penny chimed in. "I get it. The 'just' makes it sound like there won't be any problems. It *discounts* the difficulty."

"Precisely. It's what I call a 'lullaby word.' Like 'should,' it lulls your mind into a false sense of security. A better translation of 'just' in Jeff's sentence would have been, 'have a lot of trouble to.'"

"I get it," Jeff said. He came to the whiteboard and snatched the marker from my hand. Then he wrote,

> Next time, we'll [have a lot of trouble to] let you know what we really need.

"You know," he sighed, "I wish we'd had this little lesson last month. My second-best analyst up and quit on me, and I didn't see it coming. But a few weeks before, he told me, 'We haven't managed to hire another analyst yet, so I'm *just* working eighty hours a week until we do.' I should have heard him saying,

> We haven't managed to hire another analyst yet, so I'm [having a lot of trouble] working eighty hours a week until we do.

"He was trying to tell me that he was overloaded, but the 'just' lulled me into discounting his message. And, because I didn't hear him, he finally quit. Darn!"

*Soon*

Penny looked thoughtful. "I know another lullaby word that got us into trouble."

"What's that?" Jeff asked.

"You remember when we didn't have the prices ready on February first, and you asked me when we would have them?"

"Sure, but I can't remember what your answer was."

"That's because it was a lullaby. I said, 'Soon.' And what that meant was . . .'"

She looked at me, and I nodded.

She continued, almost whispering. "I think it meant, 'I don't know, but don't keep bothering me.'"

"That's usually a pretty good translation," I confirmed.

*Very*

"Actually," Jeff chimed in, "what you said was *'very* soon.'"

"Oh, great!" Penny said. "And what did that mean?"

"Adding 'very' is like slipping a sleeping pill into the lullaby. It makes it even more certain that it's going to be a long, long time. Maybe never."

We spent a bit more time discussing other examples of lullaby words, such as,

- Only: "It's only a one-line change." [That is, "I haven't thought much about what could go wrong."]

- Anything: "I didn't change anything." [That is, "I didn't change anything that I thought was important."]

- All (like "just"): "All I gotta do is . . ." [That is, "I'll have a lot of trouble to . . ."]

Eventually, I noticed that both Penny and Jeff were yawning. I suddenly realized there are many ways to put people to sleep with words, so I stopped talking and they both woke up.

Later, I reflected on the deeper lesson underlying our discovery of all these lullaby words. In effect, the words discourage feedback by putting both the speaker's and the listener's mind to sleep. When feedback is discouraged, the meaning of a statement cannot be clarified. If it's not clarified, the statement can mean almost anything—and that's always the beginning of trouble. If you want to avoid such trouble, start converting those lullaby words to alarm words—words that wake you up to potential misunderstanding, rather than lulling you to sleep. Just do it!

## CONSTANT COMMENTS

Ultimately, the most dangerous lock language comes not from clients, but from myself. In some ways, the most powerful form of lock language is a statement of the form:

I *am* a consultant.

The forms of the verb "to be" are usually at the root of what I call "constant comments" (with apologies to you tea drinkers). If you say you *are* a consultant, it sounds to me as if you're locked into consulting forever. To see the difference, compare these pairs of statements:

(a)   I am a consultant.

(b)   I am currently working as a consultant.

(a)    I am a specialist in operating systems.

(b)    One of my current specialty areas is operating systems.


(a)    I don't know how to handle such an unruly client.

(b)    Up until now, I haven't learned how to handle such an unruly client.

Notice how the (b) statements provide for the possibility that you can open some new door with your Golden Key, while the (a) statements—all constant comments—make you look and feel locked into one place forever.

My favorite Golden Key trick for unlocking these constant comments was inspired by Virginia Satir, but I dedicate it to a Nebraska farmer who was being interviewed by a reporter on the occasion of his one-hundredth birthday:

"Have you lived all your life in Nebraska?" the reporter asked.

"Well, yes," the farmer said after a moment, adding *". . . up until now."*

So, whenever you hear constant comments that seem to lock you or one of your clients into an unchangeable state, simply add, ". . . up until now." Then watch the locks spring open. We return to the power of ". . . up until now" later, in Chapter 13, when I discuss the tool that gives it strength, The Egg.

## *the courage stick*

Fear is the main source of superstition, and one of the main sources of cruelty.  To conquer fear is the beginning of wisdom.
—Bertrand Russell

The Courage Stick reminds me that I have the courage to try new things and to risk failure. Without my Courage Stick, my consulting turns to grape jelly. I refine the same techniques over and over, until all the lumps are gone. Eventually, I become too scared to try something new.

## THE COWARD'S CREDO

The first problem I'm having with this chapter is that I have no direct experience in feeling courageous. I've never done a courageous thing in my life.

My dictionary defines courage as the mental or moral strength to venture, persevere, and withstand difficulty, fear, or danger. I have overcome a number of difficulties in my life, but that wasn't courage—it was stubbornness. Facing danger is something else. Author Tom Crum defines FEAR using acronyms.[1] One of his translations of FEAR is "Fantasy Experienced As Reality," and we'll get back to that. But his definition that fits my behavior is "F--- Everything And Run." I'm a total coward, though I suppose some people don't perceive me that way. Consider these examples of what may appear to take courage:

- Admitting to my readers that I don't know much about this subject.

- Writing this chapter anyway.

These two acts may look like courage, but they don't feel that way to me. Why not?

Consider my admission that I don't know much about this subject. Many consultants seem afraid to confess ignorance on any subject, but confessing ignorance doesn't bother me. I confess it because I fear *being* ignorant and getting caught pretending I'm not. That would truly endanger my success as a consultant. So, ironically, if courage is persevering against danger, it would be more courageous to pretend I know all about courage—and to risk getting found out.

---

[1] Tom F. Crum, *The Magic of Conflict* (New York: Touchstone, Simon & Schuster, 1987).

Similarly, consider my decision to write this chapter when I don't know anything about courage. That, too, is based on fear. What I fear is not understanding the subject—so I use my Golden Key and write this chapter to learn about courage. Ironically again, the courageous act would be to abandon the writing altogether, rather than succumb to my fear of ignorance.

In spite of such reasoning, my readers continue to tell me that I am courageous for writing about certain subjects and for writing at all. Over the years, this sort of balderdash has brought me to believe in the Coward's Credo:

**Courage is not a feeling, but an outer appearance.**

I don't mean to say that there aren't people who feel courageous—it's just that I'm not one of them and I don't understand them at all. Any courage of mine you see is just an illusion, and what lies behind that illusion is usually a difference in perception or knowledge:

- a different perception of the risks and rewards of an act

- a different knowledge of the facts surrounding an act

Let's see now how The Courage Stick helps me improve both perception and knowledge.

## HOW TO USE YOUR COURAGE STICK

I tried to research courage among graduates of our Organizational Change Shop, people who have learned how to use The Courage Stick.[2] I didn't get very far, though, because most of them denied being courageous, just as I have in this chapter. So, I asked, "If you aren't courageous, how has The Courage Stick helped you?" Here are some examples of The Courage Stick in action:

- "When I found myself being afraid of how hard it would be, I used the image of my Courage Stick to remind myself of things I'd done in the past that were harder. For example, I once had four wisdom teeth extracted without anesthetic. That made this task seem trivial by comparison."

---

[2] In the Organizational Change Shop, we teach the use of the entire tool kit. Learn more about it at www.geraldmweinberg.com.

- "I was afraid the situation would come out badly, so I wasn't going to do anything. But then I touched the little Courage Stick I put on my charm bracelet following the Change Shop, to remind myself to stay calm. I started thinking of other outcomes, besides the one I feared. I saw that there were many possibilities, not just the first and most frightening one that came to my mind, and I realized that the worst one wasn't really likely, but only scary."

- "I knew that there were other possible outcomes than the one I feared, but at first I didn't think they were very likely. When I thought of my Courage Stick, I imagined myself walking into the situation with some power to act on my own behalf. Soon, I was thinking of other factors that could influence the outcome—factors that I could easily influence."

So, what in fact does The Courage Stick do? It reminds us of another meaning of the acronym, FEAR:

### FEAR = Find Every Available Resource

Once reminded of this, I shift from my paralysis into a search for other resources. I explore the facts thoroughly and consider the risks and rewards, not reacting to the first fact or risk that comes into my mind. If the risks and rewards are still unfavorable, I think of ways I can act to alter the outcomes. Having thought of all these things, I may then act in a way that seems courageous, but my action is actually the result of calm and cautious contemplation.

The Courage Stick represents the calm and comfort needed to think effectively, and the ability to handle ourselves well, regardless of what other people do. A proper Courage Stick can be held calmly and comfortably in one hand, and has no sharp points or edges. My favorite Courage Stick is a piece of wood I found on Nye Beach, in Newport, Oregon. It feels as if it were made for my hand, smoothed by countless encounters with salt waves and sand. It reminds me of how many rough encounters I have survived, and that gives me the calm to appear courageous.

Sometimes, my workshop participants suggest questionable objects to represent their courage. Some choose a large bludgeon, like a baseball bat. That image arises from the mistaken concept that courage means the ability to beat up other people.

Sometimes, people visualize their courage as a tiny pointed thing, like a needle. That image arises from the mistaken concept that courage means the ability to needle other people—to manipulate them.

Albert Einstein once said, "Great spirits have always found violent opposition from mediocre minds. The latter cannot understand it when a man does not thoughtlessly submit to hereditary prejudices but honestly and courageously uses his intelligence." That's what The Courage Stick can do—it can remind you to use your intelligence honestly, rather than simply reacting to the fears from your first prejudgment of the situation.

*The Fraidycat Formula*

To learn to look like a great spirit, you must understand how fear influences people's actions. I call this The Fraidycat Formula:

**If your fear of doing A is greater than your fear of doing B, then you do B.**

Consider these examples:

- If your fear of flossing is greater than your fear of tooth decay, then you don't floss.

- If your fear of writing is greater than your fear of not meeting the schedule, then you don't finish that report.

- If your fear of marketing is greater than your fear of poverty, then you don't make that phone call to a prospective client.

There are three different strategies for putting The Fraidycat Formula to work for you:

- You can increase your fear of B. Think about the most horrible toothache you've ever had, and the most awful and expensive dental treatment. You may find yourself flossing regularly.

- You can reduce your fear of A. Stamp the word "DRAFT" on each page of the report you're writing and plan to give it to your client "for review only." You may find you can write easily, without fear.

• You can find an option C—a third action you can take to accomplish what you're really after, an action that comes with a different load of fear. Instead of phoning the client, drop by the restaurant where she eats lunch and meet her face-to-face, as if by chance. Or send a letter, an e-mail, a telegram, or smoke signals—whatever you fear less than making a phone call.

General George Patton said that courage is fear holding on a minute longer. Use your Courage Stick to calm yourself and to remind yourself to use that minute well, finding every available resource. So, let's examine some important situations in which a consultant can use that minute well and appear to act courageously.

*Discussing the Indiscussible*

Over the years, I've come to believe that the key moment in a relationship occurs when one or both partners feel there's something that can't be talked about. This could be one thing or many things, and it could be off-limits for a lot of different reasons. When that moment arrives, the one thing that must happen is that the two partners talk about the indiscussible thing.

As a consultant, one of the most important actions I can take to improve relationships is to get that indiscussible subject out and on the table—but that can seem risky. When I begin to fear this risk, I remind myself of the terrible consequences I've seen when partners *don't* discuss a taboo subject.

For instance, I was asked to return to a company and work with Bill and Sherman, the codevelopers of a software product. They weren't speaking to each other. In this case, the thing that Bill and Sherman needed to talk about was that Sherman didn't want to talk to Bill. He didn't even want to talk about the fact that he didn't want to talk to Bill, so I decided to approach the subject indirectly, to reduce risk.

I went to see Sherman and showed him the piece of driftwood that I call my Courage Stick. I let him hold it.

"It's smooth," Sherman said. "What is it?"

"It's my Courage Stick. I brought it with me because I wanted to talk to you about something and I was a little afraid you might not like it."

*"You,* afraid of *me?"* he asked. "I've never known you to be afraid to say anything."

"Oh, I get scared about lots of things I need to say, but my Courage Stick reminds me that there are also fearful consequences when important things aren't said."

"Like what?"

"Like if I don't tell you what will happen to your company if you and Bill don't talk about some essential subjects. Like how you're going to have a product that sucks, and how everybody is going to infer that you're a lousy software architect."

You see, I didn't know why Sherman was afraid to talk to Bill, but I knew that this approach would tap into one of Sherman's greatest fears and would change The Fraidycat Formula. I never tried to get Sherman to admit that he was afraid to talk to Bill. After a little more coaxing, I led him by the elbow down to Bill's office. I stayed for a while to act as referee, but Sherman's fear soon disappeared. Later, Bill told me that it took a lot of courage for Sherman to approach him. I didn't bother to correct his impression.

## Not Giving Answers People Want to Hear

In my approach to Sherman, I used the fact that it's easy to tell people what they want to hear. We are trained in this at school and at home. Luria, the Russian psychologist, tells marvelous stories about trying to give intelligence tests to Russian peasants who did not have this kind of training.

He would hold up a picture of two adults and a child, and ask something like, "Which one doesn't belong with the others?" The peasants would answer, "They all belong. The adults are needed to work, and the child to run errands; otherwise, the adults would have to stop working."

These stories remind me of the responses I get from clients when I try to tell them about something that doesn't fit their models of reality. For example, I suggested to one client that he needed to slow down the front-end work of developing software—to take more time discovering what problem he was really trying to solve. With a puzzled look, he replied, "Apparently you don't understand the realities of software development. I've measured our development process, and we spend sixty-eight percent of our time on debugging the code. Where are we supposed to find time to do all this front-end work you're preaching about?"

Clearly, he wanted me, the expert, to confirm his erroneous model—a model that ignores the relation between his rush at the beginning and his long testing cycle at the end. And just as clearly, I wouldn't have been doing my job as a consultant if I told him what he wanted to hear. In many of my consulting assignments, I have to be the bearer of bad news—news that the regular employees don't have the nerve to report to the boss. Although it may appear to take courage, my response to the client only required a calm application of The Fraidycat Formula.

"You're right," I said, starting with what he wanted to hear. "It would be silly to add more time to the front end—*unless* we can show that it will save time in the back-end testing, where you need it most. If I can do that without disrupting any existing projects, I know you'll give me a chance to demonstrate that to you."

My client didn't want to hear that he was wrong, but he especially didn't want to hear that he wasn't the kind of guy to give somebody a chance. So, I got my demonstration, and he got a new model of how things could be done.

## Not Always Going by the Book

When you're afraid to do what's right, one of the easier escapes is to do what's conventional. As Loftus' Law states,

**Some people manage by the book, even though they don't know who wrote the book or even which book it is.**

As The Fraidycat Formula explains, when your fear of doing A is greater than your fear of going by the book, then you will go by the book. Since people are almost never punished for going by the book, a change in methods requires that the incentive for doing A must be very large, or the fear of doing A must be very small. Indeed, most people's resistance to A is simply a question of safety, or lack of it. This is why startup companies seem more courageous—they don't have the safety of a book to fall back on. And that's why you, as a consultant, can help A to happen by making it less dangerous than going by the book.

Nobody ever needs a consultant to operate by the book. People only call on you, with your high daily rates, when the book doesn't work. So, *your* Fraidycat Formula is different. If you go by the book, they won't need you and you'll lose the contract—an outcome you may fear more than anything else. This fear is the psychological basis of Marvin's Fourth Great Secret, as revealed in *The Secrets of Consulting:*

**Whatever the client is doing, advise something else.**[3]

In other words, for a consultant, this is the cowardly—that is, the safest—thing to do.

## Dealing with Impossible Demands

Sad to say, however, there's no completely safe strategy for all cases. If there were, that strategy would become "the book" for consultants—and then there would be no reason to pay us such high fees. Sometimes, the client puts on so much pressure to conform that the risk of deviation swings The Fraidycat Formula in the other direction.

For example, Johnny, a computer consultant I knew, called me for help. He had advised his client not to buy a particular software package, but then he agreed to help when the client bought the package anyway. Now the package isn't working out—and Johnny is getting blamed.

I couldn't help Johnny much at that point, but his Courage Stick could have helped him earlier. He had the courage to say what his client didn't want to hear—that the package wouldn't work—but he lacked the courage to be congruent with his earlier statement when his client asked for help. What he needed to say was, "I'm sorry, but I already told you that the package wouldn't work for you. What kind of consultant would I be if I backed down from what I said before? I will be glad to help you find some other solution, once you discover that what I said was true, if you still want me."

Johnny had been afraid to say this, for fear of seeming uncooperative. Now that he's seen the result of acting incongruently with his own judgment, his Fraidycat Formula may produce a different result next time. As Emerson said, "A great part of courage is the courage of having done the thing before." He might have added, "and discovering what you *really* need to be afraid of."

As I've learned from yielding to impossible or unreasonable demands, there's no peace of mind if you don't have what it takes to act on your convictions. The stink of cowardice is difficult to wash out of your reputation, and impossible to cleanse from your self-esteem.

---

[3] Gerald M. Weinberg, *The Secrets of Consulting* (New York: Dorset House Publishing, 1985), p. 223.

## THE COURAGE TO EXAMINE YOURSELF

Although courage may not really exist, what appears to be courage produces great quotes. Winston Churchill said,

> Courage is the first of human qualities because it is the quality that guarantees all the others.

In terms of my assessment of what's behind the appearance of courage, this would read,

> The ability to act on calm and correct assessments of risks and rewards is the first of human qualities because it is the quality that guarantees all the others.

Although my version doesn't sound as snappy as Winston's, perhaps my expression is more helpful. Most of us don't feel like the heroes invoked by the Churchills of the world, but the ability to use our Courage Sticks really does guarantee all the other tools. What good is your Golden Key if you know what doors to open or close, but are too fearful? What good is a full Wisdom Box if you cannot bring yourself to be guided by its contents? No, it's always better to be a do-something than a know-everything.

# 5

## *the wishing wand*

**What do women want?**
**—Sigmund Freud**

The Wishing Wand reminds me of the ability to ask for what I want, and if necessary, to live with not getting it. Without the ability to ask for what I want, I am powerless to be an effective negotiator. The Wishing Wand is not a *magic* wand—it doesn't ensure that I'll *get* what I want, just that I'll know what I want and be able to ask for it. Any magic that's involved, of course, arises because knowing and asking do increase my chances.

## WHAT DOES ANYONE WANT?

Freud, who understood more about people's desires than anyone of his era, was puzzled by what women wanted. Why did Freud *care* what women wanted? What did Freud want? Apparently, he wanted to understand women. Why should we care what Freud wanted?

Well, Sigmund was a consultant—a psychiatrist—and like the rest of us, he made his living giving people what they wanted, or what they said they wanted. To do this, a consultant wants to know what other people want.

What people want is no easy question. Don Gause and I wrote a rather thick book on how to find the answer,[1] and it's not the only book on the subject. Tough as that question may be for consultants, it's not nearly as difficult as a similar question: "What do *I* want?" To help you find the answer, you have your Wishing Wand.

You may have thought that once you knew how to find out what other people want, finding out what you want would be a cinch, but it's not so. We consultants are so involved in satisfying other people's wants that we tend to lose track of our own.

Here's an example. Mel owned a small consulting company—five consultants, two programmers, and one administrator—that specialized in building models of manufacturing processes. A much larger consulting company asked Mel to submit a proposal to build models for one of its clients, and Mel asked me to review his rough draft. At our meeting, I handed him a Wishing Wand and briefly explained its use. Then I went through the key provisions of his proposal, one at a time.

---

[1] Donald C. Gause and Gerald M. Weinberg, *Exploring Requirements: Quality Before Design* (New York: Dorset House Publishing, 1989).

**Jerry:** It says here that you will deliver the first model in two months. Knowing the work that you put into a model, that seems rather ambitious. Can you get that provision relaxed?

**Mel:** I don't know.

**Jerry:** Well, why do they want it in two months?

**Mel:** I don't know. It just seemed like they were in a hurry.

**Jerry:** Well, since they didn't ask for any specific time, how much time would *you* like to have?

**Mel:** Um, three months?

**Jerry:** Are you asking me or telling me?

**Mel:** Well, do you think that three months is reasonable?

**Jerry:** I'm not your customer, and I'm not you. What do *you* think is reasonable? Use your Wand!

**Mel:** Well, I suppose four months.

**Jerry:** So, how confident are you that you can build a high-quality model in four months?

**Mel:** Um, fifty-fifty?

**Jerry:** Are you asking me?

**Mel:** Well, okay, forty-sixty.

**Jerry:** So, you're saying that if you take four months, you'll have a forty percent chance of delivering a model that adequately represents your firm's abilities?

**Mel:** Yes, I guess so.

**Jerry:** Are you satisfied with only a forty percent chance? Remember, the Wand!

**Mel:** Probably not . . . but I don't want to keep them waiting too long.

**Jerry:** So, you're okay with delivering an inferior product as long as it's on schedule?

**Mel:** Not exactly. [Looks down at the Wand.] No, I guess not.

**Jerry:** So, how good would you like your chances to be? Ninety percent? Ninety-nine percent?

**Mel:** I guess I'd like them to be one-hundred percent. [Slaps the Wand into his palm, then looks away.] But you know I can't do that. Nobody can.

**Jerry:** But you'd *like* it to be, right?

**Mel:** Sure, but I have to be reasonable.

**Jerry:** "Have to" is different from "want to." Let's start with what you want, regardless of whether you think it's reasonable. Once we know that, we can start compromising with Mother Nature or with your customer. So, what you *want* is one-hundred percent?

**Mel:** [Holding up the Wand.] Sure, anybody would want that.

**Jerry:** Then why was it so hard to find out that *you* wanted that?

**Mel:** Uh, well, I wanted to be *reasonable.*

**Jerry:** Okay, so that's another thing you want—to be reasonable. We can add that to the list of things you want. The Wand doesn't set a limit.

**Mel:** But how can I have one-hundred percent and still be reasonable?

**Jerry:** Oh, I'm not saying you can *have* both—just that it's okay to *want* both.

**Mel:** But how can I ask for something that's impossible to get?

**Jerry:** Because you can *ask* for anything. That's why you have a Wishing Wand.

**Mel:** But what good is that, if I won't get it?

**Jerry:** First of all, you don't *know* you won't get it—or as close to it as makes no difference. And second, if you don't *ask* for it, you're almost sure not to get it, or even close.

**Mel:** But won't they think I'm being unreasonable?

**Jerry:** Maybe. In that case, you'll have to hear what *they* want—which may also seem unreasonable to you—and start negotiating.

**Mel:** But won't it hurt the negotiations if they think I'm being unreasonable?

**Jerry:** But you're not being unreasonable. You're just telling them what you want. Is it unreasonable to want to do a first-class job for them?

**Mel:** I guess not.

**Jerry:** So, you start out by telling them that. You say, "I'm asking for a schedule that will give me the very best chance of doing a first-class job for you—a model that fits your situation, arrives when planned, has no bugs, and can be readily modified in the future. I'm assuming that you want all those things."

**Mel:** Oh. Can I say that?

**Jerry:** I don't know. Do you have a problem pronouncing any of the words?

**Mel:** Don't be sarcastic. Of course not. But I've never started a negotiation like that before. What will they think?

**Jerry:** I can't tell you that. I'm no mind reader, especially when it comes to people I've never even met. But why do you have to know in advance? It's a perfectly reasonable thing to say, so if they react unreasonably, you'll have some information about *them*—and that's always important information in a negotiation. You can use your Golden Key to explore what's behind it.

This dialogue continued in similar fashion through the other provisions of the offer. Suffice it to say that I got Mel to triple his asking price and stopped him from offering the customer a 25 percent share of his company.

Mel seemed somewhat convinced, but still uncertain about something, so I asked about it.

**Jerry:** Are you okay with this? Is this what you want to take into the negotiation?

**Mel:** Not exactly.

**Jerry:** So, what else do you want?

**Mel:** I guess I want to be more confident about it.

**Jerry:** You seem hesitant about saying that. Why?

**Mel:** Because I don't understand how I can be more confident without offering more or reducing my requests.

**Jerry:** To want something, you don't have to know how to get it. The "what you want" comes first; the "how you get it" comes after. You seem to be in the habit of getting it backward.

**Mel:** Okay, okay. So, I want to be more confident. Are you just going to leave it there and not tell me how to get it?

**Jerry:** How would I know what would make you more confident?

**Mel:** Well, you're my consultant.

**Jerry:** Okay, then I'll use The Five-Minute Rule.[2]

**Mel:** Oh, I remember that: "Clients always know how to solve their problems, and always tell the solution in the first five minutes."

**Jerry:** Right.

**Mel:** So, did I tell you the solution in the first five minutes? I don't remember telling you anything about my confidence.

**Jerry:** Of course you did.

**Mel:** I did? What did I say?

**Jerry:** You said, "Jerry, I'm working on a really big contract, and I'm not sure I'm doing it right. Can I review it with you?"

**Mel:** But that was on the phone, before I came over.

---

[2] Gerald M. Weinberg, *The Secrets of Consulting* (New York: Dorset House Publishing, 1985), p. 67.

**Jerry:** Well, when do you think the clock starts on the first five minutes?

**Mel:** Oh.

**Jerry:** You see?

**Mel:** I see that I knew about my confidence problem, yes. But what about the solution? I don't see how I knew the solution.

**Jerry:** Well, what did you ask for?

**Mel:** I didn't ask for anything?

**Jerry:** Oh, then why are you here?

**Mel:** Oooh! Because I asked you to help me!

**Jerry:** Exactly. So, is that what you want? For me to help you in this negotiation? [I pointed to The Wishing Wand, which Mel had set on the table.]

**Mel:** Well, sure. But that's asking too much.

**Jerry:** Maybe, but how do you know that? Are you reading my mind?

**Mel:** Well, isn't it too much?

**Jerry:** That depends on what you're offering for the service— whether it's something I want. [I picked up The Wishing Wand and touched it to my heart.]

**Mel:** Oh.

After that, we negotiated an arrangement in which I would go with him to see his customer and help him hammer out a deal. During the actual negotiation with the customer, I mostly just sat there and smiled at him when he looked at me with doubt in his eyes. But in the end, he got six months to do the job and almost three times the money he was originally going to ask for—net after paying me for helping him. Best of all, the subject of giving away part of his company never even came up.

*What the Wishing Wand Can Do for You*

Let me rephrase this dialogue as a list of the reminders The Wishing Wand gave to Mel and can give to you:

1.  Don't read other people's minds; read your own.

2.  Don't worry about the feasibility of your wishes until you know what they are.

3.  Don't worry about the reasonability of your wishes until you know what they are.

4.  Don't worry about the acceptability of your wishes until you know what they are.

5.  Pay attention to what you're doing and what you're not doing, as clues toward finding what you really want.

6.  Pay attention to your feelings, as a guide to what you want and don't want.

7.  Don't worry that you might not get what you want; you'll have plenty of time to worry when and if that happens.

8.  Don't settle for less in advance of the settling.

9.  Don't set any limit on the number of things you're allowed to want.

10. Remember that you can negotiate openly with the other people involved. You don't have to do their negotiating for them. They have Wishing Wands, too.

## THE DISMAL THEOREMS OF CONTRACT NEGOTIATION

One reason The Wishing Wand is so important to consultants is that they often go as amateurs into negotiations with professionals—agencies and various other middlemen. I learned about this kind of negotiation from my friend Brad, a Los Angeles cop, when he mentioned that he regularly sells traffic tickets.

"But it's not what you think," Brad smiled. "I work at night and go to school during the day. If I have to appear in court, I miss classes. 'Selling the ticket' is convincing drivers that they really were speeding, so they won't take the matter to court."

"That's a side of police work I never considered," I said. "You have to be a good salesman."

"It's not that hard," Brad explained. "See, I give dozens of tickets every week, but most speeders only get one in a year. I get lots more practice than they do."

Negotiations between speeders and police can never be equal, because speeders are amateur negotiators and cops are professionals. By the time you have enough experience at speeding to become a professional, you'll be in jail.

Similarly, as I mentioned, negotiations between consultants and middlemen can never be equal, because consultants are amateur negotiators and middlemen, by definition, are professionals. By the time you have enough experience at contracting to become a professional, you'll be bankrupt.

Unfortunately, you do need to negotiate every new contract. So what is the best way to do that? One columnist writes,

> There will always be issues and disputes between contractors and agencies. The key, and perhaps the best that can be hoped for, is to understand the other side a little better—and then negotiate the heck out of the next deal.[3]

Although I agree that there will always be issues and disputes, I believe that the best you can do is based on understanding *your own side* a little better. Furthermore, this leads me to reinforce my previous point:

**Negotiating the heck out of a deal with middlemen is unlikely to improve your situation, because *they're professionals and you're an amateur.***

That's The Dismal Theorem of Middlemen.

But wait, things can get even worse. In order to compensate for their relatively amateurish negotiation skills, many consultants hire an agency. But the better your agency, the worse the negotiating cards are stacked against you. That's why The Utterly Dismal Theorem of Middlemen says,

**The harder you try to improve your contract by getting a good negotiator as your middleman, the worse it gets.**

Middlemen make their living by getting a high price and paying a low one. Your agency strives to get the highest possible payment from the client for your talents, but it also strives to convince you to accept the lowest possible payment for those same talents.

You may argue that your agency works primarily for *you* in that it gets a bigger cut if you get a better rate. Well, money will buy you a

---

[3] Joseph B. Darby III, "Law and Tax: It's Time to Take Non-Compete Agreements Seriously," *Contract Professional* (July-August 1998), p. 45.

pretty good dog, but it won't buy the wag of its tail. The fact that you believe your agency works primarily for you is testimony to your agency's skill at negotiation. However, that belief doesn't assure that the agency's tail wags for you. A good agency may honestly try to be your ally, but it will be opposed by the powerful dynamic of The Utterly Dismal Theorem.

Even if the agency wants to give more weight to your interests, it has to negotiate with the client. And the client, too, has more negotiation practice than you. The balance of negotiation skill will not be easily tipped against the weight of The Dismal Theorem, even if you eliminate the middleman altogether. Even though the prospect is utterly dismal, your agency may still do more on your behalf than you could do for yourself.

Paradoxically, one way out of these traps is to hire another negotiator to negotiate with your agency—someone whose *only* interest is in getting the best deal for you, not for your agency. For instance, you can hire an attorney whose fee is contingent on the quality of your deal. Such an attorney is an experienced negotiator, but not a middleman, so the sides are more even. (You can tell how strong these theorems must be if *I'm* recommending that you get help from an attorney!)

## THE HAPPY THEOREM

There is a limit to the power of the theorems, but your skill as a negotiator isn't one of them. Indeed, if you believe that you're skilled enough to negotiate with the agency yourself, you've really been "sold the ticket." To paraphrase an old saying, "Contractors who negotiate for themselves have fools for clients." Your agency may even quote this same saying—presumably without reference to your negotiation with *them*. If the agency compliments you on your negotiation skills, do not pass *ego*—get another agency!

No, the ultimate limit to these two dismal theorems is not your agency's good intentions, but, rather, your unhappiness with the deal that you've been talked into. For instance, you may feel that it's excessive for your agency to get 50 percent of each hour's pay from the client. Other contractors may be happy with the services they get for that cut of their pay, but if it goads *you*, then sooner or later you're going to leave the contract (or not renew it). Then the agency will get 50 percent of zero. I call this The Happy Theorem:

**Regardless of the agency's cut, if you're unhappy, they're impoverished.**

Unethical agencies counteract The Happy Theorem by lying or concealing their true cut of your compensation. These strategies fail miserably if you ever discover the truth. Even if their true cut seems fair to you, once it's revealed, their deceit convinces you that they're taking advantage.

Deceit is poor business, but that doesn't prevent some agencies from believing you'll never discover the truth. Some may actually try to convince you that not telling is "for your own good." Having your own skilled negotiator ensures that you'll find out—and that the agency will pay the price if it misleads you.

*Never* negotiate a deal when you don't know the client's contract with the agency! And *never* negotiate a deal with an agency if you have the slightest doubt it's being completely honest with you! That's why one of your best negotiation strategies is to talk to other contractors who have worked with an agency—before you even start negotiating.

Perhaps you believe all this, but do you really have to get a lawyer to handle your negotiations?

It's true that not all lawyers are good negotiators, and there are alternatives. Professional mediators may be a good choice, or some trusted friend who negotiates contracts for a living.

## HOW LONG SHOULD MY CONTRACT BE?

Here's a negotiation story that got great circulation among my consultant friends:

> A computer contractor died in a tragic accident and found herself at the Pearly Gates. St. Peter said, "Since you're a contractor, we're going to let you have a day in Hell and a day in Heaven before you sign a contract for eternity."
>
> The first day was in Hell, and she found herself on the putting green of a lush golf course—golf was her favorite pastime. All her old friends were there, welcoming her with open arms. She played her best round of golf ever—9 under par—and at night went to the country club, where she enjoyed an excellent steak and lobster dinner. She met the Devil, who turned out to be handsome and charming, and she danced the evening away.
>
> The next day, she spent in Heaven, lounging around clouds, playing the harp, and singing. At the end of the day, St. Peter said, "Now you must choose your contract for eternity."

*"Well," she said, "Heaven has been inspiring, but I had a better time in Hell." So she signed a contract and down she went.*

*As far as she could see, the landscape was covered with slimy, reeking sewage. Her friends were picking up the filth with their mouths and spitting it into heavy sacks slung around their necks. "I don't understand," she cried. "Yesterday there was a golf course and a country club and we ate lobster and we danced and had a great time. Now there's only endless, degrading garbage work."*

*"Of course," grinned the Devil. "Yesterday we were trying to sign you up, but today you're under contract."*

It's not much fun to find yourself condemned to a long-term contract in Hell, but your agency may think it's a great idea. Agencies generally want as long a contract as possible—to circumvent The Happy Theorem—but you may have different ideas, especially when you discover what the work is really like.

How does the agency try to justify a long-term contract? Most agencies justify their fees by the services they perform, and that's only fair. But the most costly of those services are generally performed before the contract is signed. After you've signed a contract, the agency handles tax reporting and perhaps medical insurance, but by and large, the contract's fixed percentages will more than cover such expenses. The rest, they say, is to amortize the cost of finding you a job in the first place.

If you listen to your Wishing Wand and it tells you that you value variety, what happens? You want to have new experiences, meet new people, and learn new skills to increase your value in the marketplace. Yet every time you change contracts, your agency incurs expenses; the agency makes much more money if you stay on one contract. From a financial point of view, the agency would prefer that you act more like an overpaid employee, generating the contract's fixed percentage for ever and ever.

If you want the variety, then you want a contract in which the agency percentage keeps dropping the longer you stay on one contract— eventually declining to an appropriate level for its bookkeeping services.

On the other hand, if your Wishing Wand reminds you that you prefer long-term security, you'll want a short-term contract that gives the client an incentive to hire you as an employee. Ideally, the contract would expire soon after you've proved to the client that you would be an ideal employee.

Even if you think you're too good to be an employee, you'll want shorter contracts that can be renegotiated for higher rates once the client knows you better—and once you know more about what you want. Your Wishing Wand sometimes needs some data in order to work effectively.

Regardless of the contract duration, the key to successful negotiation is knowing what you really want out of the deal. For some contractors, this is The Ultimately Dismal Theorem:

**If you don't know what you want, you're not very likely to get it.**

In the end, the only negotiation you really have to master is the one with your inner voices, using your Wishing Wand. In the meantime, since none of us knows our own desires that well, you have to resist the temptation to sign any binding contract for too long a period.

If your contract is with a company you haven't worked for, you'll have a particularly difficult time knowing what you want. For example, my friend Carla is a database consultant who trains for and runs in marathons. During a recent negotiation, she was delighted to learn that her new company had a weight room and a changing room. After she took the contract, though, she learned that she wasn't allowed to use these employee-only facilities. Fortunately, her contract was for a short project on which she could prove her value as a contractor. When she signed her next contract, she insisted on a clause that gave her access to the gym.

Over the years, I've seen many other examples in which external consultants are treated as a lower class of employee—barred from company sports tickets and picnics, relegated to park in the most distant lots, and ineligible for flextime or choice assignments.

Few consultants realize these limitations until they have signed a contract and started to work. Those who have short-term contracts are able to improve their situation on the next contract, or at worst, must endure this second-class status for a shorter term.

You need not fear negotiating new contracts. Using your Wishing Wand, you'll learn more about yourself each time, and if you do good work, you should prosper with each new deal—better pay, better assignments, better perks. And, if you do happen to make a poor choice, you won't have to spend an eternity in Hell.

# 6

## *the detective hat (and the magnifying glass)*

**It is the mark of an educated mind to be able to entertain a thought without accepting it.**
**—Aristotle**

The Detective Hat (Satir's original symbol) teamed with The Magnifying Glass (my personal addition) represent my ability to examine data (the Glass) and to reason about those data (the Hat). Without these detecting abilities, I would become a *solution-problemer*—a vendor of off-the-shelf, portion-controlled solutions—rather than a problem-solver, responding to my clients' real needs.

In a curious way, the roles of The Detective Hat and The Magnifying Glass are the most difficult to explain to consultants, because thinking and data gathering are so familiar to them. The problem that these tools solve, however, is not about thinking or data gathering. The problem concerns *remembering to do these things we know so well how to do*. In this chapter, I present a few stories about ways to remember our detective faculties.

## THE BLIZZARD OF 1969

*It was the Blizzard of 1969, and the tongues of snowdrifts lapped at our window ledges. The scene was spectacular, but Dani and I were trapped indoors for Christmas with six houseguests. We decided that if Bing Crosby could do it, we could make the best of it. The driveway was completely blocked, but we had a cord of firewood in the garage under the house, a side of prime beef in the freezer, and a rack of vintage wines in the basement. Instead of a disaster, we had a holiday party. But then the water pump failed.*

*Actually, it didn't exactly fail. More accurately, it half-failed. For some mysterious reason, the pump would run and run and run, but was unable to produce more than a bare trickle. We could melt snow for drinking, so survival wasn't an issue. Or maybe it was— without a flushing toilet, eight people can seem like a herd in a one-bathroom house.*

*Fortunately, we had three electrical engineers among us—two Ph.D.'s and an M.S. who had another M.S. in mechanical engineering. The rest of us relaxed, confidently, as one of our Ph.D.'s trudged to the cellar to "take a look."*

*After many trips up and down the stairs, many inspections, many consultations, and many theories, the pump still ran and ran and ran, and the water still trickled. The engineers were at their wits' end—and acted like it.*

*One of the nonengineers—who happened to be a potter by profession, female and blonde—suggested that "it might be a fuse." In a microsecond, her idea was pooh-poohed with the most cutting sarcasm imaginable. Ignoring these jibes, she persisted. "Why can't it be a fuse?"*

*Then followed three exhaustive explanations, at various theoretical levels, all of which amounted to the same principle: It couldn't possibly be a fuse because the pump was still operating, albeit only partially.*

*"Then maybe it's only* half *a fuse," she suggested, upon which the engineers patronizingly explained that fuses were not halfway devices. "Fuses either operate or fail. There is no intermediate state."*

*"At my house, we have fuses that operate halfway," the potter volunteered in her defense. The engineers rolled their eyes and turned their conversation to other matters. Some remarks just don't deserve a response.*

*After a few minutes, the potter disappeared. I was a bit concerned that she might be smarting from their summary treatment, so I played the gracious host and went looking for her. I needn't have troubled myself.*

*I bumped into her just as she was returning from the basement. Without a word, she went to the kitchen sink and turned the faucet. Smiling in triumph at the gush of water, she announced, "I told them it was half a fuse."*

Indeed, it had been half a fuse. More precisely, one of the two fuses that were used in the conversion of a 120 volt line to the 240 volts needed to run the pump. One of the fuses had blown, leaving the poor pump vainly laboring to draw water with half its rated voltage input. The pump ran, but it just couldn't do the job.

As it turned out, the potter had a similar arrangement at home, with her 240 volt electric kiln. Such is the value of data, and experience with data, over theory. The value of your Magnifying Glass is that it reminds you of the need to look at the data, which the engineers, steeped in theory, did not really do. They descended to the cellar and took a cursory scan only to confirm what their theories told them they should and should not see. If you refuse to see what's there, reasoning can only pump a small amount of water.

## AVOIDING DATA BIASES

As Yogi Berra once said, "You can observe a whole lot just by watching," and so reminding me to watch would, alone, make my Magnifying Glass a worthwhile tool. But it also cautions me against watching carelessly and allowing my observations to be affected by bias. We've already seen several of these situations in which somebody tries to bias the data I obtain—such as by using lullaby language or swearing that "You can trust me." When that bias is intentional, the existence of that bias may be the most important data I get. But not all bias is intentional, nor, if intentional, mischievously motivated.

Another use of my Magnifying Glass is to caution me about accidentally creating situations when I cannot possibly get the data I need. Following are some common examples of biases, most of which are created by us as observers. In each case, we must rely on The Magnifying Glass to caution us against careless observations.

## *The Railroad Paradox*

I've written elsewhere about The Railroad Paradox,[1] and since it's such a classic example of data bias, it certainly bears repeating. This paradox stems from the story about some railroad company officials who refused the request for scheduling a stop at a certain station because when they studied the situation, they found that nobody was waiting at the station at that time—when, of course, there was no reason to wait, because there was no scheduled stop at that time.

The dynamic of The Railroad Paradox is this:

1. Service is not satisfactory.

2. Because of 1, customers don't use, or underuse, the present service.

3. Also because of 1, customers request better service.

4. Because of 2, the organization denies the service request.

Overall, the paradox reduces to the following principle:

---

[1] Gerald M. Weinberg, *Rethinking Systems Analysis & Design* (New York: Dorset House Publishing, 1988), pp. 56–59.

**Because the service is bad, the request for better service is denied.**

The Detective Hat can be used to alert us to this paradoxical effect on data, so we can take preventive measures.

## The Railroad Counter-Paradox

One of my correspondents, Tim O'Flynn, wrote about The Railroad Counter-Paradox:

**When service is too good, the suppliers may never hear about it, and thus they drop the service.**

This counter-paradox should be of special interest to consultants—to good consultants, anyway. I learned about it the hard way—by not following up on some of my best clients out of fear that their silence meant they didn't like the work I'd done for them.

Fortunately, our Detective Hat reminds us that we can do something about the counter-paradox. We can solicit feedback from our clients on a regular basis, and we can search for it in more subtle ways.

## The Housewife Assumption

Another variation of The Railroad Paradox was sent to me by an anonymous correspondent. When she rang the phone company to report a buzzing sound in her phone, she asked to make an appointment so she could be home when the serviceman arrived.

"No, no," the service representative corrected her. "We'll go to your house, and if you're not home, we'll leave a card. Then you can phone for an appointment. You have to be not home in order to make an appointment."

This idiotic policy grows out of what I call The Housewife Assumption. Many service businesses base their policies on the assumption that the only important thing a woman has to do is wait at home for deliveries. This might have been true in the nineteenth century, when women were thought to be the property of their husbands. In these days of two-wage-earner and single-parent households, the probability of *anyone* being at home at some random service time is practically nil. This selection bias is important for consultants to identify because The Housewife Assumption also fails for random telephone calls to clients. In other words,

**Don't assume that your clients have nothing better to do than wait by the phone for your call.**

Again, your Detective Hat is there to remind you not to make it so difficult for yourself and your clients to provide the information you need. For instance, e-mail allows you to pass small amounts of data back and forth without having to make a simultaneous connection. And, if you must use the telephone, you can often use e-mail to ensure that you'll both be near the phone at the same time. I suppose you can use wireless phones and pagers, too, but I find that catching people unawares puts yet another barrier in the way of getting the information I need.

## SELECTION BIASES IN OBSERVATION

In some cases, you may remember to solicit or elicit data but unconsciously do it in a way that lets some kinds of data in but keeps some kinds out. Sociologist Erving Goffman writes about how this selection bias affects the diagnosis of mental patients, which is based largely on a dossier of signs of aberrant behavior:

> This dossier is apparently not regularly used, however, to record occasions when the patient showed capacity to cope honorably and effectively with difficult life situations.[2]

Unfortunately, the English language encourages this kind of selection bias—only one lie makes you a liar; one affair, an adulterer; and so on. But what are you if you go a whole day or month or year without telling a lie? We like to have predictability from the people around us, so anything that doesn't fit our model of regular behavior gets our attention, while regular behavior is ignored. This is even hard-wired into us, as I discuss with regard to habituation in Chapter 11, but it's another selection bias.

When I observe people in organizations, the same problem applies, and my Magnifying Glass reminds me to notice people's regular behavior of coping with difficult situations. My Heart, by the way, reminds me to appreciate this behavior—out loud. I'll show you how in Chapter 8.

---

[2] Erving Goffman, *Asylums* (Garden City, N.Y.: Doubleday & Co., 1961), p. 155.

*Triangulation Bias*

> *While in the midst of writing this chapter, I took a call from a consultant who wanted some coaching on presenting a proposal to a prospective client. His principal concern was that Ida, the boss who would accept or reject his proposal, wouldn't like his way of considering all sides of a question before making a commitment. We talked about all sorts of strategies for dealing with this situation, and I was about to terminate the call when my eye fell on the real magnifying glass I keep on my desk for reading 4-point type.*
>
> *"Just a minute," I said. "Where did you get the idea that Ida wouldn't like you to consider all sides of an issue?"*
>
> *"Leon warned me."*
>
> *"Who's Leon?"*
>
> *"Her administrative assistant."*
>
> *"So, you're doing all of this planning and worrying based on the word of her administrative assistant?"*
>
> *"Well, yes. Who would know her better than he would?"*
>
> *"What if he's wrong? Maybe she doesn't like it if Leon spends too much time interpreting all possible meanings when she gives him a task. Maybe she doesn't have the same criterion for consultants. Maybe she has the opposite criterion."*
>
> *"I never thought of that," Peter said, sheepishly.*
>
> *"But you told me that one of your strong points as a consultant is the way you consider all possible alternatives."*
>
> *"Yes, sure. That's why I'm so worried about what Leon told me."*
>
> *"So worried that Leon took away your power with a simple statement as a third party?"*
>
> *"Took away my power? How do you know that?"*
>
> *"Well, you didn't consider any alternative to Leon being right about Ida. You didn't think of any way to check it out. You're preparing to talk to Ida and to pretend you're not the kind of consultant that you really are. I'd say that Leon completely broke your Gyroscope, and you're totally out of balance."[3]*
>
> *"Oh."*

---

[3] For more on The Gyroscope, see Chapter 12.

*We stayed on the phone a while longer and considered a number of other possibilities. Finally, Peter hit on the radical idea that he could remove this triangulation—this third-party information—by starting his conversation with Ida by asking what style she preferred when discussing contracts. Later, he reported that she really appreciated the thorough way he explored all the alternatives in their deal, and he got the job.*

It's bad enough that you have to deal with your own selection biases with regard to another person. Adding a third party into the equation makes it almost impossible to get an accurate picture. Instead, use your Magnifying Glass to remind yourself of The Hypotenuse Hypothesis:

**When a triangle separates you from your data, choose the hypotenuse.**

A straight line is always the shortest distance to what you want to know accurately, so if you have third-party data, check it out with the party of the second part.

*The Law of the Hammer*

In *The Secrets of Consulting,* I described The Law of the Hammer:

**The child who receives a hammer for Christmas will discover that everything needs pounding.**[4]

I believe this law was originally described by behavioral scientist Abraham Kaplan as "The Law of the Instrument":

> . . . a scientist formulates problems in a way which requires for their solution just those techniques in which he himself is especially skilled.[5]

Kaplan was particularly concerned with the methods behavioral scientists used for making observations. Clearly, his caution applies to those applied behavioral scientists we call consultants.

If surveys are your strongest instrument, your data will tend to be biased toward those items that can be discovered in surveys. If partici-

---

[4] Gerald M. Weinberg, *The Secrets of Consulting* (New York: Dorset House Publishing, 1985), p. 53.
[5] Abraham Kaplan, *The Conduct of Inquiry: Methodology for Behavioral Science* (San Francisco: Chandler Publishing, 1964), p. 28.

pant observation is your cup of tea, you'll tend to get an overweighting of direct personal observations. If you're a literature searcher, you'll tend to fall victim to Weiner's Law of Libraries:

> **There are no answers, only cross-references.**

Your Magnifying Glass reminds you to spread your means of gathering information, to avoid being smashed by The Law of the Hammer.

## Fantasy Bias

The Magnifying Glass, like any tool, can be overworked. Sometimes, when data are hard to come by, I start to imagine that I know things I haven't really observed. When you're having trouble getting the data you need, as a last resort, remember LeGuin's Law:

> **When action grows unprofitable, gather information.**
> **When information grows unprofitable, sleep.[6]**

## Crisis Bias

Contrast LeGuin's Law with Crisis Bias, an approach that's often used by inexperienced consultants:

> **When in danger or in doubt, run in circles, scream, and shout.**

It's better to sleep than to get bad data, or worse yet, to create bad data yourself. If you or your clients don't follow LeGuin's Law, your data may become contaminated with Crisis Bias.

For example, you may be called only when there's a crisis, or the reports that you study may only be generated when there's a crisis. Some organizations hold meetings only when there's a crisis, so if you, as a consultant, attend meetings to observe and gather information, you're quite likely to have a biased view of that organization's life.

---

[6] Ursula K. LeGuin, *The Left Hand of Darkness* (New York: Harper & Row, 1980), p. 42.

## BUILDING YOUR DETECTIVE NETWORK

A terrific way to avoid data bias is to broaden your sources of information. Magnifying Glasses may all be pretty much the same, but different eyes see different things. Detective Hats come in many shapes and sizes—because heads come in many shapes and sizes. Much of the time, you're called upon to use your reasoning abilities in real time, right there on the spot, but sometimes your head isn't the right size and shape for the problem at hand. For these reasons, it pays to have developed a Detective Network.

It goes without saying that there is no sense trying to employ techniques over which you don't have sufficient mastery. In problem-solving, you have to start with what you know, and you're never going to know everything. But, with a network of problem-solvers at your disposal, you do know an algorithm for solving problems—namely, find someone in your network who knows how to solve the problem.

When I find myself put on the spot for an answer I don't know, I imagine that my Detective Hat is a set of Detective Headphones connecting me to my vast network of consulting colleagues. Sometimes, I can just imagine I'm talking with one of them who's an expert in the subject matter, and suddenly I know how to give a wise answer. Usually, though, I can't count on this magic consultant-to-consultant telepathy, so I buy some time and get in touch with my Detective Network by phone or e-mail or Internet forum.

I devote about an hour per day to cultivating this network and paying my dues as a resource to other consultants. It's well worth the time. I can't recall the last time I encountered a situation that stumped my whole team. One of the most important parts of my network is the Web-based forum I host called SHAPE, or Software as a Human Activity Performed Effectively. Every day, Shapers—some of the wisest software consultants from all over the world—post questions and answers in the forum for other Shapers to share. The example in the following section is drawn largely from the SHAPE forum to show you what a Detective Network—and a collection of Detective Hats—can do.[7]

## GETTING SOME GOOD OUT OF BAD INTERVIEWING

Consultants are constantly switching assignments, so they are involved in lots of interviews. One of our SHAPE forum threads was started by an independent consultant named Lynn, who complained: "I am contin-

---

[7] The *Roundtable* series of books presents excerpts from the SHAPE forum dialogues. See *Roundtable on Project Management* (New York: Dorset House Publishing, 2001) and *Roundtable on Technical Leadership* (New York: Dorset House Publishing, 2002).

ually amazed at some of the ridiculous or inappropriate questions I get when interviewed by prospective clients.  Keeping a straight face and not losing my cool is sometimes a challenge.  Any hints?"

In response, the Shapers contributed many examples from their own experiences, some of which I'd like to recount for the lessons they might offer other consultants, especially about the use of The Detective Hat.

## The Detective's First Rule

An interviewer made the following statement to Lynn:  "A psychiatrist has a model that answers to specific questions fall within.  So, by having a base model, he can identify that the problem with the marriage is the lazy wife."

Lynn, a wife herself, didn't appreciate this analogy.  One problem with this interviewer is, of course, his gender bias, which may exist throughout the company.  That problem could have distracted Lynn, but she used her Detective Hat to figure out an even greater problem: his total insensitivity to the person he was interviewing.  This is The Detective's First Rule:

**When you're looking for problems, don't be mesmerized by the first one you find.**

## The Detective's Second Rule

To be fair, however, we cannot give this interviewer the prize for total insensitivity.  For that award, I must turn to a story from a student of mine, Reva, about an interview she had with the manager of the department in which she was about to take a consulting assignment.  During the interview, he said, "I want you to feel free to come in and talk to me any time, about anything.  Think of it like a young girl talking privately to her father where she can practice her techniques for sexual advances knowing that she's perfectly safe with him, because he's her father."

How did Reva handle this?  Apparently, the same way everybody in the class handled it when she told the story—by sitting with her mouth agape for about five minutes, unable to form a coherent sound.  Then she walked away.  Maybe the manager was a masher, or maybe he was just totally out of touch, but in either case, you don't want to work for him.

Gender bias is bad enough, but maybe you're of the "right" gender. Sexual innuendo is worse, but maybe the interviewer won't find you attractive. Insensitivity, however, eventually snags everyone working in the environment, so stay away, even if you're not a wife or daughter. This is the essence of The Detective's Second Rule:

**If you're shot dead and stabbed dead, you're no more dead than if you're just shot dead.**

"Dead," of course, refers to foregoing the assignment. In other words, you don't need to justify yourself for not taking an assignment by accumulating a whole pile of reasons. One fatal reason is more than sufficient for you to depart without further explanation.

## The Nedlog Rule

As a consultant, you're sure to experience many bad interviews. You can frequently extract some good from them by using your Detective Hat to apply a variation on The Golden Rule:

**As they do unto others, they will eventually do unto you.**

I call this The Nedlog Rule. Here are some examples of verbal clues that consultants often encounter:

> **Candidate:** "So, after the merger goes through, what happens to the consultants at the other sites?"

> **CIO:** "We offer relocation to the ones we want. That's the nice thing: We can start over and define our culture."

The candidate has just learned how he will be handled should he become excess baggage. The interview continued:

> **Candidate:** "Given that, what culture would you want to have?"

> **CIO:** "That's a good question. I haven't really thought about it."

Using his Detective Hat, the candidate reasoned that the company wouldn't start thinking about its culture just because it hired him.

Here's another Nedlog example:

> **Interviewer:** "We would like to have you working for us. I already heard about you from *them*," he says, thumbing over his shoulder at the employees. "By the way, one of them, namely George, is not very productive, but I can't fire him."

This candidate put on her Detective Hat and reckoned she didn't want to be called "them," nor did she want her performance deficiencies to be discussed with actual or potential coworkers. If your clients bad-mouth other people, you have to wonder what they'll say about you.

## The Detective's Third Rule

Using your Detective Hat doesn't mean you have to use your Golden Key to get information by asking questions. Sometimes, you can learn all you need to know about the situation by applying The Detective's Third Rule:

> **Get the information you need from the questions they ask you.**

Here's a funny example. A software consultant was interviewing for an assignment in a hardware organization, but he soon discovered that its managers knew nothing about software. They asked questions like these:

- You know something about software?

- Do you write computer programs?

- Can you type? How fast?

- How long does it take someone to write a computer program?

- What's a database?

- What programming language should we use for everything?

- What's the one thing we should tell people to do to cut development costs in half?

My own answer to this last question would be, "Get rid of the managers who ask questions like that one."

So, this consultant asked himself, "Where do such idiotic questions come from? Are the interviewers idiots?" Using his Detective Hat, he tried to imagine what questions he would ask if he were going to interview, say, a brain surgeon:

- You know something about brains?

- Do you operate on brains?

- Can you cut with a scalpel? How fast?

- How long does it take someone to do surgery on a brain?

- What's a nervous system?

- What surgical tool should we use for every operation?

- What's the one thing we should tell people to do to cut surgical costs in half?

Thinking about these questions, the consultant realized that any surgeon would know instantly that he knew nothing about surgery, let alone brain surgery. The surgeon's next move should be to ask, "What is your role with respect to the job I'm interviewing for?" If there is any role at all, no decent surgeon would take the job.

Should it be any different if you're a consultant of any sort? It's not the lack of knowledge that's the problem; it's the lack of knowledge about the lack of knowledge. I can work for people who don't know beans about my specialities, as long as they know they don't know. Ignorance is curable; stupidity is fatal.

## The Detective's Fourth Rule

Sometimes, if your Detective Hat is fully employed, what the interviewer says will reveal to you that the company is not really trying to fill a position. You'll need to know The Detective's Fourth Rule:

**If you can't understand where the questions are coming from, they're probably coming from an agenda someone doesn't want you to know about.**

On our SHAPE forum, Sharon Marsh Roberts identified two common types of interviews that have hidden agendas. The first are professional courtesy interviews—ones that are scheduled because

- the interviewer owes someone a favor

- the interviewee has some (hopefully worthwhile) connections

- there is time on everyone's schedule

Sharon contrasts this to the comparison-shopper interview:

- the interviewer has someone in mind

- Human Resources hasn't approved the decision

- the corporation expects some evidence of "due diligence"

Many of the worst interviews fall into these categories, and the best thing you can do (since you'll never get the job) is save time by getting out quickly. One young consultant went for an interview believing that she was under consideration for a particular assignment. The interview started badly and went downhill fast, prompting her to ask the defining question: "Is there something that I should be telling you, to demonstrate that I can perform this job?"

The interviewer answered bluntly, something on the order of, "No, because I'm interviewing someone who isn't qualified for this position."

She gracefully departed. There wasn't much she could say, and besides, why waste more time? Sometimes, the best your Detective Hat can do is tell you when it's time to leave.

## The Calming Effect of Wearing a Hat

For the consultant who's wearing a Detective Hat, interviewers reveal this kind of information in dozens of other ways. No matter how inept an interviewer may be, you can almost always get the information you need to make a decision.

But in each of these instances, the first reaction of the consultants being interviewed was to get very *angry*—and thereby to lose their ability to reason about the significance of the data they had just obtained. Eventually, each of them calmed down and thought about what useful meanings they could extract from the information. That's what The Detective Hat does: It reminds you not to lose your head—and your Hat along with it—and not to lose the meaning for which you paid with so much emotion.

## The Detective's Fifth Rule

In Sir Arthur Conan Doyle's detective series, Sherlock Holmes had a less famous brother, Mycroft, an armchair detective who apparently never left his gentleman's club. Mycroft was smarter than Sherlock, and he applied pure reason to the extent that Sherlock used a variety of tools for investigation. But ultimately, Sherlock was the better detective. Mycroft relied too much on reason alone. Your Detective Hat is but one tool in your kit, and like any tool, its use should not exclude the use of others.

In *The Secrets of Consulting,* I present three principles that are known as Sherby's Laws of Consulting. My colleague Bob Wachtel, who knew Sherby personally, reminded me that Sherby had a fourth law—one that I had forgotten—probably because Sherby's Fourth Law is about overusing your thinking prowess:

**If you're using anything more than fourth-grade arithmetic, you're probably doing it wrong!**

Even if you're doing it right, you'll still have to convince your clients that it's right, and this takes fourth-grade arithmetic, at most. After all, at least one out of three published math papers contains some error, even after review by some of the world's finest mathematicians.

Most consulting problems are not very deep, intellectually. As they say out here in New Mexico, where I spend most of the year, "It don't take a genius to spot a goat in a flock of sheep." Or, as Dani's dog-trainer colleagues say, "The nose is smarter than the brain. Ask any dog."

Ted Williams once said,

**If you don't think too good, don't think too much.**

Ted was one of the greatest hitters in baseball, and his rule probably kept him from trying to outthink the pitchers, which is a losing game. The pitcher's job is to confuse the hitter, to get the hitter thinking rather than batting. In consulting, your clients may create confusion because, on some level, they don't want you to solve their problems. They may prefer to have the problems they know than the problems that will rise to the top once you solve their biggest one.[8]

So, when you're confused and tempted to start thinking too much, think about applying The Detective's Fifth Rule:

> **Confusion favors the established order, so use your confusion to find the culprit.**

Confusing tax laws favor the rich, who can afford tax specialists. Confusing corporate rules favor corporate executives, for those who would change the established order risk breaking some rule they don't understand. As a consultant with a Detective Hat, you may be able to cut through all that confusion by applying The Detective's Fifth Rule to find the culprit—who could turn out to be the executive who hired you.

---

[8] This statement is a variation on Rudy's Rutabaga Rule: "Once you eliminate your number one problem, number two gets a promotion." See *The Secrets of Consulting,* p. 15.

## *the yes/no medallion*

If they were women, they'd all be pregnant.  They can't say no.
—Pat Schroeder, Congresswoman from Colorado,
commenting on how her colleagues appropriate money.

The Yes/No Medallion is a metaphor for my ability to say yes, my ability to say no (thank you), and my ability to mean what I say. Without a yes that truly means yes and a no that truly means no, I would pander to my clients' prejudices and my advice would be worthless. The Medallion represents my ability to choose, including my ability to choose not to choose, for now.

But perhaps you're wondering why I need such a reminder. What is it about yes and no that's so hard to pronounce? Or, if I can't say them in English, why not in other languages—oui, non? ja, nein? da, nyet?

For me, the difficulty with giving a clear yes or no comes from two sources:

a.     I may want to pretend I'm not making a choice, so I don't want to say yes, which would make me responsible for choosing.

b.     I may not want to hurt the other person's feelings, so I don't want to say no.

Let me tell you a story about my trouble with item b.

### THE CHAPTER FROM HELL

Nobody's perfect. Sometimes, you have to make mistakes if you want to improve. Anyway, that's my excuse for once serving a few years as a college professor. But don't let anybody tell you different—there are many things you can learn in college. Consider this lesson I learned during my tenure as a professor:

> *One warm day in late April, I was gazing enviously out my office window at all the students taking advantage of spring in the ways that college students are inclined to do. Suddenly, a short, energetic fellow with a bushy black moustache swept into my office and introduced himself as Professor Myron, from the business school. Shaking off my reverie while shaking his hand, I heard him say*

something about having me write a chapter for a book he was editing.

*Ah, I thought, this is a no-brainer.* I knew all about edited collections and the chapters in those collections, and I didn't want any part of one, under any circumstances, especially when I didn't care for the topic earmarked for me. All I had to do was find a polite way to say no without hurting his feelings. No sense making enemies, especially on campus.

"Oh," I said, trying to sound sincere, "it sounds like such an interesting project. When is it due?"

He lowered his head apologetically. "Well, I know this isn't very nice, but I've already submitted the manuscript. You see, I had all the other chapters ready, but my publisher said the book just had to have this one more chapter. So, that doesn't leave you very much time. I'm sorry, but I need it by June, at the latest."

What an easy setup—a ready-made excuse that took advantage of his guilt about asking me so late in the game. "I'm so sorry, but I'm just totally committed to other projects until well into the summer."

His shoulders drooped, and he sighed audibly. "I'm not really surprised. I should have given you more warning."

That was so easy, I couldn't resist laying it on a bit thicker. "Yes. I couldn't possibly do a project of such importance until September, when I'd have had my whole summer to dedicate to it." I stood up and patted him comfortingly on the shoulder as I guided him, dejected, out of my office so I could return to the birds and bees.

I had done such a fine job, I thought, that I put the whole matter completely out of my mind—until two weeks later, when Professor Myron bounced into my office again. As soon as I saw the smile on his face, I knew I was in deep trouble.

"Guess what?" he said.

"What?" I replied, not really wanting to hear his answer.

"I called my publisher, and he said that since a chapter from you would be so important, he'll hold the project until September!"

*I did a lot of thinking between the next two breaths, trying to come up with a different excuse. Perhaps I could tell him that I'd committed to another project just last week, and now my plate was full until November—maybe until next year. But then his publisher might delay again, and how long could I keep using the same phony excuse?*

*At that point, my Wisdom Box whispered in my ear, "You fool. You need a lesson that you'll never forget, and this is your big chance."*

*So, I simply smiled at Professor Myron and said, as graciously as I could muster, "Why, that's wonderful. I'll devote my whole summer to it." Which I did.*

*Every darn day during that long, long summer, I dragged that manuscript out and added a few tortured words, words that seemed written in my own blood. And, every darn day, my Wisdom Box would whisper, "You're going to remember this, aren't you, next time you ought to say a simple no?" Which I did. For the rest of my life, so far, at least.*

Back then, I didn't even know I had a Yes/No Medallion, nor would I have known much about using it effectively. If I had, the story would have been much shorter and very much sweeter. Had I known about Satir's Soft Spurn, there would have been no Summer of Suffering at all.

## SATIR'S SOFT SPURN

After the Summer of Suffering, I rarely forgot *when* to say no, but it was many years before I learned *how*.

My initial process for saying no was simple: Somebody would offer me an assignment that I didn't particularly want, and I would recall the Chapter from Hell. I would remember how angry I had been at myself for accepting the assignment. Then, when my anger reached the boiling point, I would blast the requester with superheated steam—something like, "You've got a lot of nerve, asking me to contribute my time to a dumb project like that! Get out of here before I really lose my temper!"

Needless to say, nobody ever asked me twice, which wasn't such a fine outcome when business got slow. I began to realize that I was losing friends and potential clients, but I didn't know any other way—

until the day I overheard a guy named Larry offer a truly ridiculous assignment to Virginia Satir.

"Why, thank you, Larry," Virginia said, gently touching his arm and looking warmly into his eyes. "I'm honored that you would ask me. Unfortunately, it doesn't fit for me at this time." That was the end of the interaction, but it wasn't the end of her relationship with Larry, who walked away beaming with disappointment.

Over the years with Virginia, I had the opportunity to watch her use many variations on her soft way of spurning unwanted offers. Here's the recipe I extracted from all these examples:

1.  Show genuine appreciation, in words, tone, and body language (for example, saying, "I'm honored that you would ask me . . .").

2.  Give a regretful but clear no, without excuses (saying, "Unfortunately, it doesn't fit for me . . .").

3.  Indicate an opening to some other relationship in the future (saying, ". . . at this time").

In short, if you don't want to do it, simply say it doesn't fit. Don't make excuses. But if you really would have liked to do it, give your excuse and keep the relationship open for a similar request in the future, saying something like this:

> I'm honored that you would ask me. What a shame that I'm fully booked during the next three months. But please ask me again if this comes up again after that.

My biggest barrier to applying Satir's Soft Spurn was the requirement for genuine appreciation. I knew I couldn't make an appreciation sound sincere if I really didn't value what was being offered. I asked Virginia about this, and she confessed that she often didn't appreciate what was being offered.

"But, I always appreciate their offering it to me," she said. "It's like your grandson offering you a dead frog he just found in the mud. It's not the gift that counts, but what it means for the giver to offer it to you." This is putting your Heart into the equation, as I discuss in Chapter 8.

Now, imagine I had known about Satir's Soft Spurn when I was approached by Professor Myron:

**Prof. Myron:** "Jerry, I'd like you to write a chapter for my forthcoming collection of papers."

**Me:** "Well, thank you, Professor. I'm very flattered that you'd invite me to write a chapter for your book. Unfortunately, the project just doesn't fit for me at this time."

**Prof. Myron:** "Oh." [Here, I escort the professor out of my office.]

End of story. No Chapter from Hell, no Summer of Suffering.

## GORDON'S LAW OF FIRST CONSULTING

The Medallion, of course, is not just a No Medallion. It also reminds you when to say yes. Saying yes to the giver, rather than to the gift, is just the first of many applications. Another example is what my pen pal, Gordon Schaffer, calls Gordon's First Law of Consulting, but which I prefer to call Gordon's Law of First Consulting:

**Don't say yes to a client's first offer, but never say no.**

It's called the Law of *First* Consulting because this is one of your first interventions as a consultant. Whatever you say or do at the opening gun sets a precedent for what happens during the whole race.

So, what do you say when a potential client offers you something that your Wisdom Box says doesn't fit for you? Satir's Soft Spurn can be a model here, too, but instead of the no, you want to say something totally noncommittal that also acknowledges receipt of some information and the opening of a valuable relationship. I like to say,

"Oh, thank you for that offer. Let me think about it and get back to you."

What I've said is yes—not yes to the offer, but yes to considering the offer. Now I can take some time to think clearly, not under pressure, and come back later to share my thoughts on the matter. Perhaps it's not the right kind of work for me, or the conditions for success are absent, or possibly the compensation isn't right.

But what if the client insists on an answer right now? Another possible response is,

"Well, let's go over that again to make sure I understand exactly what you're offering."

This transforms a demand into a negotiation. It's still not a yes to the offer, but a yes to trying to understand the offer. Even if you don't love the proposal, perhaps with a few negotiated modifications you can learn to live with it.

But what if the client insists that you accept on the spot—with no discussion, even if you don't understand it? Well, then your job is easy:

> "I really appreciate your offering that. Unfortunately, such a quick decision doesn't fit for me at this time."

This, to any but the most dense, is a polite but clear way of saying no to a client you wouldn't want to do business with—unless the client backs down and says yes to giving you more time.

## SAYING SIMPLE YEA AND NAY

The Bible is quite clear on the subject of The Yes/No Medallion: Everyone should have one. The Book of Matthew puts it this way:

> But I say unto you, Swear not at all; neither by heaven; for it is God's throne:

> Nor by the earth; for it is his footstool: neither by Jerusalem; for it is the city of the great King.

> Neither shalt thou swear by thy head, because thou canst not make one hair white or black.

> But let your communication be, Yea, yea; Nay, nay: for whatsoever is more than these cometh of evil.

This is wise advice, whether you're the speaker or the listener. Beware of people who try to make their yea or nay stronger by swearing:

> "As God is my witness, I'll deliver that report on time."
> "I really mean I'll do it."
> "Don't worry, I won't accept his offer."
> "Trust me. I am not a crook."

Here's what I call Matthew's Yea/Nay Signal:

> **Honest, reliable people don't need to qualify their yeas and nays with declarations of their honesty and reliability, and everyone instinctively knows this.**

When you catch yourself appending one of these self-advertisements to your clear yea or nay, it's time to take a look at what's going on inside. Chances are, you don't trust yourself, and you're trying to put your clients to sleep with the lullaby words we discussed in Chapter 3.

## YES, NO, AND SURVIVAL RULES

In my experience, most consultants have more trouble using the No side of their Medallion. Our aversion to saying no is often rooted in the rules we learned as children, rules that are so deeply ingrained that we perceive them as necessary for our very survival.

In the course of training consultants to use their Medallion, I often gather lists of survival rules. A selection of some of the most common rules from these lists may give you an inkling of why survival rules choke our throats when we try to say a perfectly reasonable no:

- If you don't have anything nice to say, don't say anything.
- You must take care of everybody.
- Never insist on getting your own way.
- Don't disagree with an authority figure, especially your mother.
- Don't talk back.
- Don't deliver bad news.
- Don't fight or argue.
- Anything you do, do perfectly.
- Be good.
- Always cooperate.
- Always give people the benefit of the doubt.
- Don't say something you'll regret later.
- Don't make a scene.
- Always keep the peace.
- Don't get caught in the middle of a conflict.
- Always be considerate.
- Never hurt anyone else.
- Always be kind and helpful.
- Respect your elders.
- Don't rock the boat.
- Don't let anyone else get angry.
- Pretend to be happy.
- Treat girls with respect.
- Treat boys with respect.
- Be considerate.

- Don't be selfish.
- Don't say anything that might cause pain.
- Don't tell people your problems.
- Always participate.
- Always be helpful.

If you have children, you'll recognize many of these rules because you use them to make your children easier to handle, and heaven knows, parenting is hard enough. But when you see the whole list laid out like this, you can begin to imagine why it's so hard for those children, now supposedly grown-up consultants, to say no to just about anything. The overall impression is, "I'm not entitled to say no, and nobody will like me if I do."

If you try to live by this impression, you won't have any time left to be an effective consultant, so follow The Goody Goody Guide:

**If you *must* have *everyone* like you, get out of the consulting business.**

*Transforming a Yes Rule*

My survival rules are central to the way I participate in interactions. Rules are not to be thought of as bad; on the contrary, I honor my rules for helping me to survive this long in a difficult world. By honoring my rules, I acknowledge that they may need to be updated to fit the changing world. What fit for a four-year-old preschooler may not fit a forty-year-old consultant.

But what's wrong with rules for an adult is that they don't use my Yes/No Medallion. They are all absolute and offer no choice, no chance to say yes or no. That's why, if I'm to have a fully functional Medallion, I need to consider transforming some of my rules into guides.

By transforming a rule into a guide, I retain the old possibility but add a few new ones—giving me a choice in place of compulsion. For instance, take the common rule, Don't deliver bad news. Analytically, I can see that this may block my being a good consultant, but emotionally I certainly would like to deliver good news all the time. When the rule is transformed, I can deliver good news when it is appropriate and be free to deliver not-so-good news when that is more fitting.

The rule is transformed by the following steps:[1]

---

[1] For more on survival rules and rule transformation, see Gerald M. Weinberg, *Quality Software Management, Vol. 3: Congruent Action* (New York: Dorset House Publishing, 1994), and Gerald M. Weinberg, *Becoming a Technical Leader* (New York: Dorset House Publishing, 1986).

1.  State the rule precisely, starting with "I must always": *I must always deliver good news.*

2.  Change "must" to "can": *I can always deliver good news.* Ask yourself, Is it true?

3.  Change "always" to "sometimes": *I can sometimes deliver good news.* Ask yourself, Is it true?

4.  Select three or more circumstances in which the guide can be followed:

    *I can deliver good news when*

    - *I don't have to lie to do it*
    - *there actually is news*
    - *there actually is good news*
    - *what may seem bad to me might be good to someone else*

Most project managers I work with would be delighted if they and their team members could transform the rules that prevent them from saying no when they think it would be "bad news." They could then count on honest feedback to use in steering their projects through all the inevitable bad news—news that gets even worse when nobody will tell you about it.

### Transforming a No Rule

There are also a few rules about when it's not okay to say yes, and similar transformations can be applied to those, to activate my Medallion. For example, consider this rule I had as a youth:

**Never accept charity.**

For years, my strict application of this rule required me to say no to any sort of gift offered by a client—even corporate marketing baubles, such as pens, paperweights, belt buckles, and project T-shirts. When such things were offered to me, I would stiffen mysteriously and refuse as politely as I could manage. Nobody failed to notice my body language, and it didn't endear me to my best clients. Imagine how you'd feel if someone you considered a colleague stiffly spurned a small token offered out of friendship.

*My haughty behavior ended when Sylvia, a colleague I shared a condo with at one of Virginia Satir's month-long seminars, offered me a handmade macrame scissors tail. A macrame scissors tail? My amused curiosity was so strong that my Golden Key took over and seized control from my No rule. What in the world was a macrame scissors tail, I wondered, and why would I want to have one?*

*Sylvia showed me how the colorful, knotted cord attached to a scissors handle with a clove hitch.*

*"But what does it do?" I asked.*

*"It makes it easier to find the scissors in your sewing drawer."*

*"But I don't have a sewing drawer," I said. My No rule was trying to reassert itself.*

*"Okay, but you have a desk drawer, don't you?"*

*"Yes," I had to admit.*

*"Well, this is a desk-drawer scissors tail, because I made it especially for you. Actually, I'm kind of new at this macrame stuff, and this is the simplest project in the book. I've already made two of them for myself, but this is the first one good enough to give as a gift. I knew you'd like it—and they're surprisingly helpful."*

What could I do? Something had to yield, or I would crack. Fortunately for me, we had been working on rule transformation that week, so I captured my "never accept charity" rule and transformed it into the following guide:

> *I can accept charity when*
> - *I feel the offer is genuinely free of obligation*
> - *I sense a friendly intent behind it*
> - *the gift is not something I couldn't afford for myself*
> - *I don't really need the gift*

## The Stuck Medallion—Rule Conflicts

Sylvia helped me change by putting two of my rules in direct opposition—"Never accept charity" and "Never hurt anyone's feelings." In my own life, and among my clients, I have found numerous such rule conflicts. I list some of them below, divided arbitrarily into columns for Rule 1 and Rule 2:

| Rule 1 | Rule 2 |
|---|---|
| Always be honest. ............ | If you can't say something nice, don't say anything. |
| Plan ahead. ................... | Don't count your chickens before they're hatched. |
| Don't make mistakes. .......... | Don't be afraid to take a risk. |
| Don't get your own way. ........ | Don't let anyone take advantage of you. |
| Don't ever go away. ............ | Grow up. |
| Don't be loud. ................ | Speak up. |
| Learn as much as you can. ...... | Don't study all the time. |
| Don't hide your feelings. ....... | Don't ever show that you're hurt. |
| Stand up for your rights. ........ | Don't disagree with an authority figure. |
| Don't linger at the table. ....... | Don't rush through your food. |
| Don't go hungry. ............. | Don't eat just before going to bed. |
| Don't brag. .................. | Speak up for yourself. |
| Find work; stick with it. ........ | Don't put all your eggs in one basket. |
| Make the world better. ......... | Leave things as you found them. |
| Work for what you want. ....... | Don't be selfish. |
| Don't be shy. ................. | Don't be loud. |
| Be a team player. ............. | Do not depend on anyone else. |
| Don't be prejudiced. ........... | Marry your own kind. |
| Be forgiving. ................. | Never forget when someone does you a wrong. |
| Be perfect. .................. | Don't act like you're better than other people. |

Little wonder that such rule conflicts would paralyze my Medallion at the most inopportune moments. As Rule 1 would start to say no, Rule 2 would interrupt and start to say yes. But before that yes could emerge, Rule 1 would seize control again. While the two rules played tug-of-war in my head, I would freeze with a half-witted look on my face—not a very reassuring consulting posture.

Once I learned to transform my survival rules, I welcomed these moments. The hidden rules they surfaced could now be transformed into guides, and my Medallion could once again perform its essential service. Similar transformations are effected by another tool, The Gyroscope, as I discuss in Chapter 12.

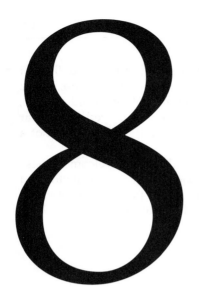

## *the heart*

If love is judged by its visible effects,
it looks more like hatred than friendship.
—La Rochefoucauld

$\mathbf{T}$he Heart represents my ability and willingness to put heart into my work, and to do it intelligently, rather than just with good intentions. My colleague Jean McLendon introduced The Heart to my kit, though she claimed that the only reason Virginia didn't have one in hers was that she assumed everyone always had access to their heart. Working in technical environments, though, I've learned that I often need to be reminded of the hopes and wishes and fears and sensitivities of others. The Heart gives me that nudge when I need it.

## HEART TROUBLES

You've probably heard that heart disease is the number one killer of consultants (and other people). But did you know that Heart troubles are the number one killer of consulting practices? Throughout all stages of my career, I've been plagued by Heart trouble of various kinds. Since I've observed others with these same symptoms, I suspect you may also be at risk.

The Heart is in my tool kit to remind me about *my own personal values*. But one of the worst Heart troubles of consulting is to impose your values on your clients, so I won't hold forth on my personal value system in this chapter. Just as you'll find my Wisdom Box contents throughout my books, you'll find my Heart there, too.

Instead, this chapter shows *how* to use The Heart—not what you should be using it for—and how to avoid some of the Heart troubles that have affected my consulting practice.

## *Heart Boomerangs*

Hearts are dangerous. Perhaps of all the tools in the kit, The Heart is the most likely to produce boomerang effects—the exact opposite of what it's supposed to do. For example, my Heart reminds me that I value X, so I take some action to make X happen, and the result is that the opposite of X happens. Think about pulling off a large bandage. You don't want to hurt the patient, so you pull it off slowly and carefully—but this only extends the torture.[1]

---

[1] If you'd like to read more about boomerang dynamics, see Gerald M. Weinberg, *Quality Software Management, Vol. 1: Systems Thinking* (New York: Dorset House Publishing, 1992), pp. 278–86.

Here's a common example of a boomerang in organizational life: being indirect as a way of not hurting people and winding up hurting them. In our SHAPE forum, a new contributor named Vlad wrote a bunch of questions that some of the veteran contributors didn't understand. Several of them wrote to me privately about the questions, rather than communicating directly with Vlad. They were using a style that was different from the usual SHAPE style—some level of indirectness with someone they don't know (or don't know well) to avoid hurting his feelings. I don't expect everyone to understand that mode, but it arises out of motives that are just as pure as those who confronted Vlad directly.

To respond to those Shapers, I pointed out that indirectness to avoid hurt can also lead to hurt, in certain situations. I asked, "How would you feel if you were Vlad and discovered that others were corresponding about your contributions, but leaving you out of the correspondence?"

In the context of the SHAPE forum, I felt the indirectness worked adequately because people could write to me and count on me to help out—because that's one of my jobs as forum editor. But don't get in the habit of relying on third parties to take care of these difficult interpersonal situations. Consider this an application of The Hypotenuse Hypothesis:

**When a triangle separates you from your data, choose the hypotenuse.**

This transforms into The Human Hypotenuse Hypothesis:

**When one person, C, separates your heart, A, from another's, B, choose the shortest path between A and B.**

But it's The Heart itself that prevents us from going directly to the source. The people who wrote to me were in a genuine quandary—they valued Vlad's contributions enough to want to understand them, but they really didn't understand what they didn't understand. And they valued Vlad sufficiently that they didn't want to hurt his feelings. Their Hearts seemed to recommend the indirect route. What else could they have done?

More importantly, what can you do when you find yourself in a similar situation? Your Heart yearns for one outcome, but anything you do in that direction seems to risk having the opposite effect.

What I've learned to do in those situations is tell the other person, directly, "I'm really interested in helping you out, but I don't understand what you're asking, and I don't even understand what I don't understand. Can you help me to help you?" This works better in face-to-face conversations; it's a bit too slow for print or especially e-mail.

A different instance of this Heart boomerang can occur when your Heart indicates that you don't really value your relationship with a certain person. You don't want to continue spending time with them, but you don't particularly want to hurt them. You try to let them know in a gentle way, but they interpret your gentleness as the main message—a message that says you really do value your relationship with them.

Again, it's like pulling the bandage. If you try to avoid hurt altogether, you're likely to cause more problems than you solve. The Heartful approach is to be as clear as you can, using your Medallion, saying that you want to wind down the relationship. But how can you be as clear as you can, when Hearts are involved?

## THE INFORMED HEART

One of the heartwarming benefits of writing a book is all the lessons I learn from my readers. Here's part of a letter from a reader named Larry, who had just praised *The Secrets of Consulting:*

> There was one section that caught my attention, because you were telling about having a difficulty I've never run into: getting people to be aware that they have feelings. As an assistant trainer of Neurolinguistic Programming (NLP), I help people to have more choice about their feelings, or to refine their perceptions of them, and while this can be a challenge, no one has ever objected that they didn't have feelings.

I guessed that Larry doesn't work with computer programmers, as I do, for I've frequently heard them claim they don't have feelings, or if they do, that they aren't important. Of course, that makes Larry's advice all the more useful. He continues:

> I think I can help you to get people to access their feelings more readily. (I realize that this violates The Fourth Law of Consulting, but consider it an application of The Seventh Law of Marketing.[2])

---

[2] The Fourth Law of Consulting: If they didn't hire you, don't solve their problem. The Seventh Law of Marketing: Give away your best ideas. See Gerald M. Weinberg, *The Secrets of Consulting* (New York: Dorset House Publishing, 1985), pp. 9, 176.

*The first thing I noticed was the large number of visual words you use in this section, e.g., getting people to "see inside themselves," referring to them as "blind to feelings," giving them a "first glimpse." Figures of speech that involve visual words tend to get people to process information visually. Conversely, having someone "get in touch with" or "contact" their feelings, even if they have to "grope" (not search) for them, will lead toward a kinesthetic (feeling) processing. Even when dealing with physical feelings, it's more effective to "move" your attention to your left foot than to "focus" your attention there.*

*One more suggestion: If someone is stuck or confused in thinking about what they're feeling in the present, it's often helpful to get them to access past feelings, for example, "Remember a time when you were angry, or nervous, or in love. How does that compare with what you're feeling now?"*

I wrote to Larry, giving special thanks for his information about getting in touch with feelings. Even though I've trained as a master practitioner of NLP, and I was a student of Virginia Satir, from whom it all started, I repeatedly fail to apply what I know about NLP. When I am working, my use of auditory, visual, and kinesthetic language sometimes slips back into unconsciousness. Larry's letter reminded me that I have to *tune in, watch* my step, and *be more on top* of things. (How's that, Larry?)

I especially depend on an *informed* Heart, one used in a *conscious* way, when I write. If I'm not in touch with my readers' difficulty in understanding, not attuned to their sensory preferences, and not able to see their response, I easily slip into language that suits my sensory preference for visual communication but fails to make contact with them.

I have to use the informed Heart when I speak, too. Some of my colleagues tend to be unresponsive to any form of spoken interaction about feelings. I empathize with them, because not very long ago, I was the same—my Heart was locked away, protected from any further pain. In such cases, I try to touch the person, literally, and I find that appropriate nonverbal contact often starts to open the path to the person's Heart (thus confirming Larry's insight).

When touch is not available or too intrusive, I can sometimes speak more or less directly to a person's unconscious, bypassing their conscious barriers, using The As-If Technique:

**If you *did* have feelings, what would they be like?**

If that doesn't work, then I try another approach:

**What kinds of feelings do you think other people have?**

The As-If Technique works by offering people some safe distance from their own feelings. It doesn't require them to expose their feelings in public—which may have caused them pain in the past.

The As-If Technique gets to The Heart of some of the hardest cases, but like virtually all of my techniques, it won't succeed unless it comes from my Heart. I firmly believe that my *informed* Heart, the combination of my head (technique) and my heart (caring), is what produces any consultant power I possess.

Throughout my career, when I've used my Heart in an uninformed way, I've gotten into big trouble. Let me give some examples.

## Mindless Conformity

At the beginning of my career, I was naturally eager to attract and retain clients, and I thought this would only be possible if they loved me. Like a teenager, I felt that conformity was the surest way to get people to love me. So, I tried to be as much like my clients as I could. I dressed like them; I used their jargon; I worked their hours; I concerned myself with the same problems.

At first, because I shared the same background as many of my clients, I didn't notice my pattern-matching behavior. But I did notice how many times my clients tried to hire me as an employee. Eventually, I figured out that if I was too much like them, they couldn't figure out why I wasn't an employee. Then they would wonder why they needed another employee at higher prices.

I reacted by going to the opposite extreme, trying to be as different as possible—in dress, speech, thinking, and attitude. It took me a few more years to figure out that I was frightening clients away. My nonconformity caused the fear that I might actually do something different from what the employees were doing.

I was caught in The Parallel Paradox, a nifty double bind:

**If you're too much like your clients, you don't attract them; if you're too different, you frighten them away.**

So, how did I escape? I discovered that it's much easier to just be myself. For one thing, it takes much less calculation. But being myself does require some very hard work—learning to know my true Heart.

## Mercy Consulting

When I started consulting, I believed that once I had an established reputation, my worries would be over. I would be deluged with requests for my presence, so I could pick and choose my assignments. And, I had a pretty good idea of my true Heart—what I really wanted to do.

However, once I was established and started getting three or four times the number of requests that I could satisfy, I still felt that I was wallowing in one miserable assignment after another. After a few years of such misery, I finally had the sense to ask some of my consulting colleagues for help, during a lunch break at a conference. The men in the group weren't much help, but the women instantly recognized the phenomenon.

"It's like high-school dating," said Martha.

"How so?" I asked. "I don't know much about high-school dating. In high school, I was such a nerd I couldn't get anyone to date me at all."

The women all turned to Anne, the most physically attractive of the group, and she answered immediately.

"There are lots of nerdy boys in high school," she said. "It probably comes with the age. They're driven by their hormones to approach girls, and if you're a moderately attractive girl, you're deluged with requests for nerdy dates."

"But you can just turn them down," I said. I knew they could, because I was always turned down, but I didn't want to admit it to them.

"Well," said Anne, "you turn *most* of them down, but eventually their pitiful condition gets to your heart. So, you grant a mercy date— and you almost always suffer for it." Some of the other women nodded in agreement.

"Nobody ever granted *me* a mercy date," I complained.

"Maybe you weren't pitiful enough," Martha said, and I decided to take that as a compliment. "However," she continued, "some of your clients *are* apparently pitiful enough for a mercy date from you. Like that company that . . . "

"Whoa!" I said. "I don't want to discuss my clients' problems."

"There you go," Martha admonished, "spreading mercy again."

"Well, then let's change the subject," I suggested. Mercifully, they did, but my mind wouldn't abandon the concept of the mercy date.

Late that sleepless night, everything came clear. I realized that when my calendar availability was limited, I chose assignments by reasoning according to the following algorithm:

- If a sound, sensible client invited me to work with them, I concluded that they didn't really need my help that desperately, so I would decline the offer.

- If a truly pitiful client invited me, I concluded that if I didn't help them, nobody else would. Although I didn't think I could help them succeed, I could help them feel better about their failure. So, I would accept the offer.

Until that night, I hadn't been aware that I was applying this algorithm and taking on these mercy cases. Although I had learned how to use my Yes/No Medallion, I hadn't learned to use my Heart in an informed way.

Nowadays, if a client in a pitiful situation invites me to work, I center myself by getting in touch with my respect for the people involved, first as human beings, then as human beings who are feeling serious distress. Then, I always offer my heartfelt caring, because I do care about them, just as I care for every human being.

I listen from a caring center, and I accept their state, no matter how sorry it seems. But this acceptance doesn't imply either my approval or my future participation. It's not for me to judge the client, but it is for me to judge whether or not trying to help the client fits for my Heart.

Instead of offering just any kind of help, I suggest some simple step we both can use as a measure of whether or not their situation is truly beyond my power to help. For instance, I often suggest that they send a couple of their most influential employees to one of our leadership workshops. If they cannot manage to do that—too busy, too cheap, not sufficiently confident in me, too unaware of the potential benefits of improved leadership, or unable to identify any influential employees—then that's the end of it.

If they do send some of their best people, then we have, in effect, a very short and risk-free consulting contract. I can get to know their people and at the very least send them back to the office with some tools for assessing and improving the situation. Once in a while, the relationship grows into something much bigger than that.

That's what happened for Anne and Martha. After our group discussion, they confided that they each eventually married the winner of a mercy date—and lived happily (and reasonably) ever after.

One of the benefits of inviting prospective clients to workshops is that I don't have to assess the organization over the telephone or via e-mail—which would amount to a blind date. Also, I can use this approach with every prospective client, satisfying my Heart's desire to treat everyone—nerd or prince—with equal respect.

MAGNIFICENT COMMITMENT

The Heart is, or should be, the motivator behind everything I do. If my Heart isn't in it, I shouldn't do it. I ensure this with The Heart Test:

> **If you don't care about them or their problems, don't consult for them.**

Through bitter experience, I've learned that when my Heart isn't in it, I don't do my best job. And if I don't do my best job, I don't get follow-on business or referrals. Clearly, I have to pass The Heart Test to succeed as a consultant.

But passing The Heart Test is not sufficient to guarantee success. It took me a long time to learn that treating everyone with equal respect is not the same as treating everyone. Time after time, my Heart led me to overextend myself by trying to take care of everything for everyone. And what a noble position that was—I might not have been helping anyone, but I was willing to die trying. Also, this stance was perfectly safe, for although people might criticize my work, nobody could ever criticize my intentions.

I kept up this noble position until the third time I came close to dying from overwork. Then I finally figured out that I was a person, too, and if I wanted to care for everybody, I had to care for myself. Now, I live by a different credo, The Life Law:

> **Better to live succeeding than to die trying.**

So, sometimes, even when my Heart *is* in it, I don't do it. My Heart is not infinite in capacity. If it's acting in an informed way, my Heart reminds me that I must have boundaries. Otherwise, my Heart will burst. I call this The Informed Heart Test:

> **If someone requires you to die trying to help them, you don't want to help them.**

# the mirror

Oh wad some power the giftie gie us,
To see oursel's as ithers see us.
—Robert Burns, "To a Louse"

The Mirror represents my ability to see myself and to seek and use feedback. I'd always known that feedback was important to personal growth, but I learned much more about it as I worked with Edie and Charlie Seashore on our book about feedback, *What Did You Say?*[1] Feedback is the mirror in which I can see myself and monitor how I am affecting those around me—but it only works if I remember to look in the mirror that other people offer. For any individual or organization to improve, this feedback is essential.

Being a mirror includes acting congruently, so as to be a non-distorting mirror, for others, and in order for you to interpret what comes back. This is easy to say, but hard to do. It's a bit easier when I have a little time to reflect, rather than give my first reaction—impulsive and probably incongruent—to feedback that doesn't sound flattering. The Mirror in my tool kit reminds me to wait a bit before I respond.

Of course, when the feedback concerns my writing, it's easier to get time to reflect accurately. Here's an extended example, based on feedback I got from a column I wrote on the slippery subject of commitment. A reader, Brad, wrote a letter to the editor of the magazine, showing me how poorly I'd communicated the meaning of "partial commitment" to him.

My first reaction was, naturally enough, to try to blame this miscommunication on Brad: "He must be a careless reader, or something," I thought. But my Mirror reminded me that it's my job, as author, to make myself clear. So, I applied a Mirror trick I use when I catch myself blaming, The Three-Finger Rule:

**When you point a finger at someone, notice where the other three fingers are pointing.**[2]

So, I looked more closely at Brad's feedback as an example of what it can do and how to use it.

Here's part of what Brad had to say:

---

[1] C.N. Seashore, E.W. Seashore, and G.M. Weinberg, *What Did You Say? The Art of Giving and Receiving Feedback* (North Attleboro, Mass.: Douglas Charles Press, 1992).

[2] Gerald M. Weinberg, *The Secrets of Consulting* (New York: Dorset House Publishing, 1985), p. 66.

*Weinberg's approach is to minimize his commitment to a troubled project until the client has proven its commitment to Weinberg's strategy for making the project successful. He writes, "If, as time goes on, the organization proves true to their word, I may increase my involvement." This approach is ludicrous on two counts: One, most contractors don't have the luxury of choosing to make a partial commitment to a project. We do one gig at a time—for us it's all or nothing, and a "partial" commitment means "partial pay."*

Here, my error was in choosing the term "partial commitment," which was too easily mistaken for *"part-time* commitment." (I'll quote his second count further down.)

When I make a part-time commitment, it's always a *full commitment for what I've promised to do,* as are all my commitments. What I mean by a partial commitment is that I don't initially agree to do every job a client asks me to do. Instead, I make a *full commitment to part of the job offered.* Here's an example:

*Monica was an expert in testing. Company X wanted her to act as test manager for a troubled project, from start to finish. But she knew that Company X had a habit of cutting the testing at the end of projects in order to save its schedules—and then blaming its test managers for the poor quality they delivered.*

In response, Monica offered Company X a partial commitment. She would fully commit to lead the test planning and also to participate in the project planning. She would also commit to assist the company in searching for a permanent test manager. If the management failed to hire one in time, she would negotiate further commitment—based on how well the project had been managed at that point.

## BEING A MIRROR

The Mirror in my tool kit isn't just about using one. It's also about being one. Offering such partial commitments is a powerful form of feedback that alerts companies to things they need to change. Offering such feedback is part of the job of every professional who provides a service. For example, if I go to my doctor with back pain, she doesn't just give me painkillers for short-term relief. She also gives me exercise, posture, and movement guidelines that will help me prevent future pain. A doctor who fails to be this sort of Mirror is not doing a full, professional job.

For consultants, contract negotiation is a great opportunity to offer feedback, because contracts are powerful Mirrors. When you enter a negotiation, remember Monica's Marvelous Mirror:

**Negotiating a contract is a marvelous opportunity for both parties to take a good look at themselves.**

Monica's contract negotiation alerted Company X to their nonproductive behavior, and they improved in the early project stages. Monica was willing initially to negotiate a new contract—a commitment to stay until the first components were delivered for testing. Suddenly, though, Company X reverted to its old pattern. Monica was told that although the components were not ready for testing, the testers would have to keep to the original schedule and cut three weeks off the test allocation.

Since Monica wasn't committed to continue under any circumstances, she was able to use her negotiating position to gain a schedule change and restore the originally planned testing. In the end, Company X delivered a stable product. It was three weeks late, but nobody blamed the testers because Monica's accurate feedback had forced them to realize just where the delay originated.

Of course, not all contract-time feedback has such a happy ending. Monica's Mirror is marvelous, but not miraculous. Not every patient follows the doctor's advice, and not everybody likes what they see in The Mirror—*especially* when The Mirror is perfect. Even though using The Mirror may mean turning down work, in the long run, it helps you, the consultant, when your Mirror is unblemished.

Monica had previously used the partial commitment approach with a different client—and with different results. When an extension to the contract was due, the client refused to accept her conditions, so she had to seek a new client. This might seem like a good reason for hiding your Mirror from the client, but as Monica told me, "I was there every day, and I could see what was coming; so, I had some prospects lined up. The day my contract ended, I got a new contract to manage some testing for a client who really appreciated what I had to offer. I'm sure I was much happier there than I would have been on the death-march project that ensued at the first client. Paid better, too. And maybe the old client will learn something and change, but I wouldn't bet on it."

That's another lesson, which I call Monica's Mirror Monition:

**Some people do not wish to look in a marvelous mirror.**

*Sweeny's Teeny Weeny Signature Statute*

Of course, Monica's story may not address Brad's second point:

> *. . . clients don't typically go out of their way to prove any commitment to a contractor. In fact, one could argue that clients use contractors precisely because they need to make absolutely no commitment to us at all!*

I know what Brad means—some clients (not all) will promise anything to get you to take an assignment and then will default on those promises. Using feedback through partial commitments is precisely the strategy to protect your interests when you fear that a client isn't going to honor commitments, even those in contracts. Here is an example:

> *Sweeny took a software development contract with Company A, agreeing to stay until the project was finished. He was told that the project was under great pressure, that there would be extensive overtime, and that he would be paid $80 per hour for regular time and $120 per hour for work exceeding 40 hours per week. When he opened his first paycheck, however, he had been paid a straight $65 per hour, even for his 14 overtime hours. His project manager explained that upper management had decided the rates were too high. The figures quoted in the interview, he said, were "only an estimate, anyway, not a commitment."*

How did Sweeny react? Not wisely, in my opinion. He stayed until the project was finished (months late) because he felt "committed." For me, a commitment is also partial in the sense that I don't have to do my part if my clients don't do theirs. Consultants who submit to this kind of shoddy treatment are failing to give feedback to their clients, and this encourages those clients to continue dishonoring their commitments.

Of course, Sweeny had no written contract, because he didn't like what he called "legalities." On his next project, though, I did convince him to use a contracting firm as an intermediary, and that firm, at least, honored its verbal contract with him—though I'm not so naive as to believe that all contracting firms meet their verbal commitments.

All parties to a contract need feedback in order to improve, and the best way to ensure that feedback is to use a written contract that *both parties sign.* Monica's Marvelous Mirror may not always work with verbal contracts, but it's very effective with written contracts: There's something about signing your name to a piece of paper that makes you actually look at your commitment. I call this Sweeny's Teeny Weeny Signature Statute:

**If you want a meaningful commitment, don't whine, sign.**

### The Helpful Model and Carl's Constructive Corollary

Carl was also a software developer on a contract, but his contract was negotiated through a contracting firm. He told the agency he would only commit to implement a single, specified module, even though the client wanted a commitment throughout a project of unspecified length and scope. Once he went to work, he discovered that he was required to share an inadequately provisioned workstation with another contract developer—and then was berated for working too slowly. Since his contract had not explicitly specified that he would be given the proper tools, he was caught in this revolting situation—but only until the committed module was finished. He didn't renew.

Instead, he got a new contract with a new client, and this time his contracting agent investigated the working conditions a little more carefully—having learned from feedback. Carl also made sure he had the protection of a partial commitment. This client fulfilled its part of the bargain, and Carl renewed. After four years, he's on his sixth contract with this client.

In his letter to the editor, Brad called attention to the difficulty of applying the partial commitment approach:

> *Perhaps there is an elite class of contractors who can successfully employ Weinberg's approach. But for those of us in the trenches, priority number one is unquestionably this: Keep busy. This is not avaricious; it's pragmatic.*

I would amend Brad's statement, for myself, to this:

> Keep busy doing work you do well and enjoy, under proper working conditions, where you are respected and have a chance to show yourself at your best.

And, yes, there is a class of consultants who can employ this professional approach, though I wouldn't call them elite. Many of them are my students and colleagues, and I'd definitely call them pragmatic. They know that whether feedback helps them win or helps them lose, feedback can always help them learn.

For feedback to work, they have to set aside negative interpretations of why they were given the feedback and apply The Helpful Model:

**No matter how it looks, everyone is trying to be helpful.**[3]

Remember, that "everyone" includes you, and so on both sides of The Mirror,

**Use feedback as a reminder, not a reproach.**

This application of The Helpful Model is appropriately named Carl's Constructive Corollary. It works even if the feedback was not actually *intended* to be helpful—in which case, it's a way to turn intended harm into a potential benefit.

Brad, of course, didn't intend to harm me with his letter to the editor. How do I know? He opened his feedback by saying, "Normally I love 'The Big Picture,' and Gerald M. Weinberg's insights into the world of contracting." This is an exemplary feedback technique because this comment aided me in interpreting Brad's other comments as attempts to be helpful, not as attempts to try to harm me in some way. This comment also ensured that I would pay some attention to the rest of his comments, which were not so easy to accept because they told me what he didn't like.

Ironically, Brad showed me that he was only "partially committed" to my columns, and thereby offered me feedback by which I could improve my writing. I'd say that makes Brad both pragmatic and professional, and a Master of The Mirror.

## Kenny's Law of Auto Repair

Sometimes, it's difficult to angle your Mirror properly to reflect on what's wrong. This is a special instance of Kenny's Law of Auto Repair:

---

[3] See Gerald M. Weinberg, *Quality Software Management, Vol. 1: Systems Thinking* (New York: Dorset House Publishing, 1992), pp. 154–55, and Gerald M. Weinberg, *Quality Software Management, Vol. 3: Congruent Action* (New York: Dorset House Publishing, 1994), p. 208.

**The part requiring the most consistent repair or replacement will be housed in the most inaccessible location.**

Similarly, the part of you that needs the most constant repair or consistently causes trouble will be the part that's most inaccessible to you. It's the part for which you most need your Mirror—and the part that your Mirror is least likely to see.

Your Mirror may not be able to see what may otherwise be an obvious part of you. It's similar to the feeling you get when you forget a name or a word that you otherwise would instantly remember. Sometimes, a word can lose its meaning if you stare at it for too long. One summer, forgetting a word almost got me killed.

Many, many years ago, four of us teenagers went on a road trip across America, but at a certain point, we almost ran out of money and had to drive nonstop back home to Chicago. We took turns driving, sleeping (sort of) in the car to conserve what money we had left for gas. One night, we were driving through a muddy detour in Arkansas, and I was navigating—which mainly consisted of keeping the driver awake and reading signs for him. After many miles down a dark farm road, I saw a strange sign with a word on it—a word I couldn't read or even pronounce. The word was STOP.

The message that I needed was the one I couldn't read, and my inability to read it should have given me the same message.

That kind of blockage often happens in life. Sometimes, the inability to get the message *is* the message—and the *most important* message. It tells me about my own state of consciousness. My own Mirror is at fault, but I often blame my inability on another person or on the context.

So, where do we look to find out about our own internal states? What is the secret of introspection, of seeing ourselves as "ithers see us"? To find these secrets, I examined the sciences that study human behavior.

Psychology was the first discipline I investigated, only to realize that modern psychology often scorns introspection and has become the study of *other people's* behavior. This chapter on using The Mirror—how I look to myself and how I feel inside—is not science as psychology defines it.

I next turned to sociology, but sociology is about the *mass* of other people's behavior, not about me, the individual.

What about history? History is about how people *used to* behave, interpreted through the perspective of how the mass of people behave today.

Anthropology? That's about how *really different* people behave—and so, for that matter, is psychiatry. Studying the insane isn't going to help me use The Mirror on myself, unless I want to drive myself nuts.

Each of these scientific approaches offers me distance and safety from dealing with myself, but ultimately, I am the only person I can really change. As the Zen master Shunryu Suzuki says, "If someone is watching, you can escape from him, but if no one is watching, you cannot escape from yourself."[4]

So, Secret Number One is this:

**There are no secrets. Everyone can observe human behavior.**

It takes no more equipment than you already own. And you don't need a research grant.

## SATIR'S THREE UNIVERSAL QUESTIONS

My editor at *Contract Professional* chose the name for my monthly column, "The Big Picture." He told me he chose the name because I "look at the business of contracting and consulting and the people skills involved, which translate across all skill sets and even industries"—in short, The Big Picture.

That's flattering—but why would you want to look at the Big Picture? If you're like me, you're often called into an assignment because you're supposed to be an "expert." You know what an expert is: "someone who avoids all the small mistakes while committing a grand blunder."

My preference, though, is to understand The Big Picture. So, before I get down to the nitty-gritty of a new assignment, I like to place everything in a grand array. I always make many mistakes in my assignments, but with The Big Picture, I can hope they'll all be *small* mistakes.

My favorite method of approaching The Big Picture is first to break down the question into three parts: self, other, and context. In this chapter, of course, I've started with my self, which is where I always start in consulting. The self perspective uses The Mirror.

---

[4] Shunryu Suzuki, *Zen Mind, Beginner's Mind* (New York: Weatherhill, 1960).

Focusing on my self, I then ask three questions I learned from Virginia Satir:

- How do I happen to be here? (Past)
- How do I feel about being here? (Present)
- What would I like to have happen? (Future)

Here are some examples of Big Picture questions that help me look in my Mirror and that make an enormous difference in how I approach an assignment.

*How Do I Happen to Be Here? (Past)*

- If it's my first assignment with a client, how did I make the connection? Was it through a third party, or by direct contact from the client?

- If it's a repeat, what impressions did I leave on my previous assignments? Did I leave friends, or enemies? Are my old contacts still viable? What assumptions am I carrying from the previous assignments?

- Did I get the contract I wanted, or did I have to make some concessions that may come back to haunt me?

*How Do I Feel About Being Here? (Present)*

- Am I here reluctantly? Do I have some reservations or forebodings about this assignment?

- Am I eager to be here? Am I looking forward to the task that I've agreed to do?

- Am I puzzled about what's expected of me, or is the assignment clear? How sure am I of the assignment?

- How sure am I of myself—of my ability to provide value in exchange for value received?

- However I'm feeling, is this the right mood for succeeding in this job? If not, what steps will I have to take to get in the right mood?

*What Would I Like to Have Happen? (Future)*

- Why did I take this assignment? For the money? The experience? The challenge? The possibility of a future reference? If I don't have my mission in mind when I choose a course of action, the client may be happy with my work, but I'll come away with a hollow feeling.

- What will success look like, to me? If I come away with a pile of money but a poor reference, will I be satisfied? How about an ecstatic client who's enormously impressed with a solution I've repeated so often it bores me into a trance?

- How long do I want to be here? If the client extends the project, will I be laughing or crying?

## USING THE BIG PICTURE OF YOURSELF

By using these three questions as a Mirror before I start an assignment, I increase my level of satisfaction enormously. I use these questions to survey my state before I agree to any contract, new or renewed.

On one occasion, for instance, I was about to renew a long-standing contract with a nice 15 percent increase in my daily fee. When I checked my feelings, though, I realized that I had negotiated for the wrong thing. On the previous contract, I felt that I was doing a fine job at solving the wrong problem, and I didn't find that very satisfying. I didn't mind the extra 15 percent, but what I really wanted was more involvement in defining my own assignments.

Armed with improved self-knowledge, I halted the negotiation process and asked for more leeway. I was prepared to sacrifice at least some of my increase, but the client granted me more latitude and insisted on the higher rate. He said, "Now that you'll be helping us do the right things, rather than just doing things right, you'll be worth at least that much more to us."

Self-assessment doesn't always pay off this directly. On another renewal, early in my career, my attempt to get more leeway in defining my work led to an irreconcilable difference between me and my client. This client knew—or thought he did—exactly what his problems were, yet I felt his poor problem definition limited my ability to be successful in my terms.

At that time in my life, what I wanted most was experience with certain types of problems and a few outstanding references. On my first assignment with this client, I helped solve a problem that didn't involve the kind of work I really wanted to do. Although my solution was innovative and successful, I felt that it didn't really help the client with his true problem—since he was working on the wrong problem to begin with.

He attributed his lack of satisfaction to some unspecified shortcoming in my work, and he was reluctant to give me a sterling reference.

And, of course, he was right. The shortcoming in my work was my failure to look in my Mirror and to assess The Big Picture—both his and mine—before I took the assignment. As we negotiated for a follow-on, Satir's three questions showed me that the extra money he offered wasn't adequate to overcome my bad feelings about working with him again. Negotiations broke down, but at least I didn't waste another six months of my life struggling for something I didn't really want.

It took me a few weeks to get a new assignment, and that cost me a few bucks. The cost is long forgotten, but I still savor the memory of my satisfaction with the new assignment—what I learned, what I earned, and how it put my professional life back on my own track. As the Chinese proverb says, "We cannot prevent birds from flying over our heads, but we need not let them nest in our hair."

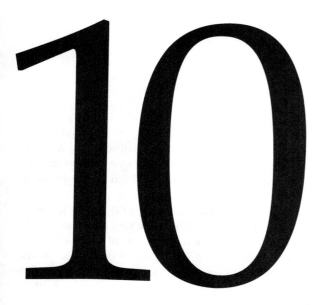

# 10

## *the telescope*

The definition of a beautiful woman is one who loves me.
—Sloan Wilson

In human intercourse the tragedy begins, not when there is misunderstanding about words, but when silence is not understood.
—Henry David Thoreau

The Telescope reminds me of my ability to see others and to bring them closer to my understanding than my naked eye and brain can manage. My Telescope is a pair with my Mirror, which reminds me to see myself.

Suppose you're entering a new situation and you'd like to garner a Big Picture of the other people involved. Whatever you do, don't try to use The Telescope without first getting a Big Picture of yourself. You need to ask yourself the Three Universal Questions I described in the last chapter. If you're not personally centered with a personal Big Picture, the techniques I'm about to describe may seem overwrought or even smarmy.

## WHICH OTHER PERSON'S BIG PICTURE?

Although The Mirror can only be used on one person, my Telescope can target billions of people at once. How do I decide where to aim it?

I start each assignment by asking myself, "Who will the significant others be in this context?" Anyone I omit from the scope of my vision may appear in the lens at a critical juncture and spoil my best-laid plans.

The people I usually have to consider are Dani, my wife and business partner; Sweetie and Ruby, my German Shepherd dogs and biggest supporters; Lois and Susie, my coworkers; other colleagues in my network, such as my workshop and conference faculty associates; and my clients, the people who pay my bills. In this chapter, I focus on this last group, especially the people I work with on an assignment.

## LOOKING AT SATIR'S QUESTIONS THROUGH THE TELESCOPE

As I do when I use my Mirror, I use my Telescope to look for the answers to Satir's Three Universal Questions:

- How do they happen to be here? (Past)

- How do they feel about being here? (Present)

- What would they like to have happen? (Future)

Let's see how these questions helped me start on the right foot at one company, even when presented with a bad beginning.

Soon after I arrived at the organization, one of the first comments my client, Isabelle, volunteered was, "We've had consultants before, but none of them made any difference." I'd heard remarks like Isabelle's before, and for many years, they put me on the defensive. Fortunately, at this time, I had learned to apply The Helpful Model and to assume that Isabelle was trying to be helpful. Having centered myself that way, I simply asked myself, "What does this mean, and what should I do about it?" Let's see how the three questions can help me.

## How Do They Happen to Be Here? (Past)

When Isabelle raised the issue of past consultants, she gave me a head start on answering the questions I use to guide my discovery of the client's past:

- Did Isabelle choose to be here, or was she forced by me, or by some other party, such as her boss?

- What is her history on this job? What knowledge does she have that I can tap into? What prejudgments has she made about the nature of this task?

- Has she had prior personal or cultural experiences that may affect the way she works on this job? With me?

- What's been her past experience with me or with other consultants? What preconceptions does she bring to the table as a result of these experiences?

These are not excuses for poor performance, but things I have to understand in order to work well with Isabelle.

## How Do They Feel About Being Here? (Present)

In this instance, thanks to Isabelle, I knew right away that this organization "had consultants before, but none of them made any difference." Obviously, Isabelle felt that this was an important thing to say, but I didn't know why she brought this up so early in our relationship. To find out, I asked myself questions about the present circumstances:

- Does Isabelle have some reservations or forebodings about this assignment? About me? Does our doing this assignment conflict with something else she wants to do?

- Is she eager to be here? Is she looking forward to working with me on this task?

- Is she clear about what's going to be required of her if I take the assignment?

- How's her self-esteem? Does she feel able to control her situation and accomplish her personal goals, or does she feel powerless?

- However she's feeling, is she in the right mood to help me to succeed in this job? If not, what steps can I take to help her get into the right mood?

I often seek this information by asking, "And what does that tell you about my tour of duty?" Here are some of the answers I've received from various people, at other times when my tour of duty followed a consultant's failure:

**Aaron:** "You don't have a chance, so I'm not going to waste any time helping you."

**Bonnie:** "You're going to need my help if it's going to turn out differently this time."

**Carter:** "It's nothing personal, but this is going to be another of those management vision things, full of sound and fury and going nowhere."

**Darleen:** "I'm really excited, because you're different from any of the consultants we've had before. This time, our consultant is really going to make things better around here."

Each of these answers is full of information that directs me to work differently with each of these people.

*What Would They Like to Have Happen? (Future)*

Before I started to work with Isabelle, I had to know the answer to the third question:

- Why did Isabelle agree to work with me on this assignment? The experience? The challenge? Fear of her boss?

- What will success look like, to Isabelle? Is that aligned with my success criteria? Did previous consultants solve problems that she failed to solve, thus making her look like a failure?

- How long does she want me to work on this assignment? Will I be able to stay long enough to see it through? If the customer extends the project, will Isabelle be laughing or crying?

To find answers to these questions and to respond to Isabelle's comment about previous consultants, I remembered what I had said to Aaron, Bonnie, Carter, and Darleen. In those cases, I assumed they genuinely hoped something would change, but I knew that each felt differently about my involvement. I tried to use their comments to open a discussion to get at what they would like to have happen:

To Aaron, who said "You don't have a chance, so I'm not going to waste any time helping you," I said, "I can understand your feeling. I'll do my best not to waste any of your time, but if I should happen to come up with something that might save you some time, would you be interested in hearing about it?"

To Bonnie, who said "You're going to need my help if it's going to turn out differently this time," I said, "Great! What sort of help do you think you can give me?"

To Carter, who said "It's nothing personal, but this is going to be another of those management vision things, full of sound and fury and going nowhere," I said, "Yes, I've sure seen my share of futile, grandiose projects. I personally think that big changes result from an accumulation of small changes. Would you be willing to work with me on some small change that would help you in some way? Then we could see if we're wasting our time, or if things might be different this time."

To Darleen, who said "I'm really excited, because you're different from any of the consultants we've had before. This time, our consultant is really going to make things better around here," I said, "I'm flattered. Thank you. In what way do you think I'm different from the others, and how do you think that will help?"

As a result of learning their Big Picture, I'm no longer knocked off balance. Instead, I'm well centered and already beginning to create a method of working appropriately with each of my clients.

## THE RESPONSE PATTERN

When I demonstrate the way I use my Telescope, fledgling consultants often ask me, "How do you come up with such responses in real time? They make sense when I read them, but in the moment, I often go blank."

There is a pattern to my responses, and I'll describe it here, but it won't work if you think of it as a formula.

First, since I have to remain creative in order to complete the pattern, the first thing I must always do is center myself. I use my Mirror and my Gyroscope, which I discuss in Chapter 12.

Next, I find a way to connect with the *emotional content* of what the other person is saying, relating my own emotional state to theirs. I learn about this emotional content from the second Universal Question, "How do you feel about being here?"

Last, I proceed to the content—what the person wants to have happen—and I decide what steps I can take to move the situation toward what they want.

We'll see this pattern repeatedly. I've taken it from aikido, the Japanese art of harmonizing energies.[1] The pattern is called "center-enter-turn":

1.  First, *center* yourself.

2.  Second, *enter* the other person's emotional system.

3.  Third, move to problem-solving that will *turn* the situation.

If you skip the first step, you won't be able to use The Telescope and enter the other person's emotional system. If you skip the second step, your move to problem-solving will usually fail—unless you've managed to enter their emotional system by accident.

---

[1] For more on aikido, see J. Stevens, *The Secrets of Aikido* (Boston: Shambhala, 1995).

*The Telescope Focusing List*

This pattern of center-enter-turn sounds rather simple, in the same way that a telescope is intuitively simple to use. But just as telescopes go out of focus, so does our ability to truly see and hear the other person. Virginia Satir had a checklist of things that put us out of focus when we're looking at another person—things that we can correct, just as we can learn to correct the focus of a telescope if we know what knob to turn. She called this checklist, "With whom am I having the pleasure—you, or my picture of you?" I combined her list with some new items to produce my Telescope Focusing List, which includes the following items to check:

1. *Centering.* What frame of mind am I in? Am I aware of my mental and emotional processes? Am I totally here, in the present? What's my emotional and physical state? Am I experiencing discomfort that distracts me? Is some pain (even a message from my bladder) grabbing my attention away from the person I'm with?

2. *Environment.* What's really here, now? What are the environmental conditions in which this observation takes place? What is the overall situation in which we're doing this? Am I looking/seeing, listening/hearing, touching/feeling what's actually here? Or am I remembering other times, other places, other people? Do I have certain expectations or prophecies or hopes that are coloring my observations?

3. *Recording.* What would a camera see in this person? Am I seeing and hearing what a video camera would record—that is, description with no interpretation whatsoever?

4. *Resemblance.* Whose hat did I hang on this person? Who does this person remind me of? Is her voice like my former girlfriend's voice? Is his nose like my dog's? Does she dress like Queen Victoria? Does he pound on the table like Nikita Khrushchev?

5. *Projecting.* Are these thoughts and feelings really coming from the other person, or am I using the person as a projection screen for my own thoughts and feelings? Am

I asking leading questions that increase my chance of getting back what I believe I'm going to get back?

6.  *Pigeonhole.* What categories am I applying? That is, what preset ideas do I have about the identifiable groups this person belongs to? "Tall women are domineering." "American Indians are peaceful and noble." "Protestants are bigots about Catholics." "Men with thick glasses are good lovers." Even if I believe that a stereotype is generally true, does that stereotype have any bearing on this relationship?

7.  *Mind Reading.* What do I imagine is going on in the other person's head? In particular, what do I think she thinks about me? Am I more concerned with what she's thinking *about me* than what she's thinking? Do I need to remind myself that the last thing someone will be thinking about me is that I'm no good? That's what I fear most often, and so that's what most distorts my sensory apparatus.

8.  *History.* What experience, if any, do I have with this person, good or bad? Does any of that really apply here and now? Is it really relevant at this moment that he once tripped in the cafeteria and spilled green chile chicken soup down my back?

9.  *Hearsay.* What third-party information did I bring to this encounter? What have other people told me, good or bad? Is it gossip? Even some wonderful story? Is there some reason I can't check it out rather than rely on indirect information of unknown veracity?

10. *Sharing.* How do I feel about sharing the items on this checklist with the other person? Do I feel I have permission to speak the unspeakable?

When something goes screwy, I check my Telescope Focusing List to debug the interaction and bring it back into focus. I ask myself The Data Question:

**What specifically did I see or hear that gave me that impression of this person?**

When I discover that it's not the person that's out of focus, but something in me, I bring it up.

But can I bring it up? Item 10, on sharing, is in some ways the most important. After all, if I'm not willing or able to share some item, how can I check out my Big Picture? To keep my Telescope in focus, I always check the last item first.

# 11

## *the fish-eye lens*

Intricate patterns of effective behavior have grown around the lessons of success and failure, creating a Gordian Knot of Corporate Normalcy. . . . Every new policy is another hair for the Hairball. Hairs are never taken away, only added. . . . The Hairball grows enormous.
— Gordon MacKenzie
*Orbiting the Giant Hairball*

The Fish-Eye Lens represents my ability to see the context—what surrounds you and me, influencing us as we work together. It's my third visual tool: The Mirror helps me look at myself; The Telescope helps me understand the other person's perspective; The Fish-Eye Lens shows me the combined perspectives of everyone involved. For a consultant with auditory preferences, the corresponding tools might be the tape recorder, the hearing aid, and the omnidirectional microphone. The Fish-Eye Lens reminds me to use the many observational and analytical tools I already possess, many of which I've written about yet fail to recall when I most need them.

## ISABELLE'S INITIAL INDICATION

Remember how Isabelle, soon after I arrived at her organization, volunteered, "We've had consultants before, but none of them made any difference"? I remember her; in fact, I always have Isabelle on my mind when I enter a new consulting situation, because she reminds me that

**You never start with a blank slate.**

I call this little reminder Isabelle's Initial Indication. It urges me to retrieve my Fish-Eye Lens and start looking all around me. *All* around me.

And why do I need a reminder? Because if I had my druthers, I'd always start my consulting with a blank slate. Then I could center, enter, and just commence turning, willy-nilly, without ever encountering any unanticipated side effects of my interventions. I wouldn't really have to design custom interventions, since my client would have no history.

Unfortunately, this is a fantasy, sometimes called The Green Field Fantasy, based on the notion that it would be easier to build buildings if you always started from a green field, nice and flat, just growing clover. That never, never happens. I need a Fish-Eye Lens to tell me why this field, this client, this context, is different from every other I've ever seen or will ever see again.

THE LAW OF UNAVOIDABLY MESSY PECULIARITY

Then again, perhaps each client is not *entirely* different from every other one. My Fish-Eye Lens reminds me that I have a head start in determining context because some parts of it are fixed. These fixed parts are best seen with a set of lenses that are bundled into my lens bag under the title of general systems thinking, a collection of laws that form part of the context of *any* situation.

For example, all my clients are human beings (so far), and they all have brains. Moreover, they're all dealing with immensely complex systems that they must simplify if they are to understand anything at all. In this, they are driven by The Lump Law, which we saw earlier, a very strong general systems constraint that arises from our own mental limitations:

**If we want to learn anything, we mustn't try to learn everything.**[1]

In computing, certain mathematical transformations are employed to simplify calculation. Underlying these transformations is the idea that certain computations are stronger, or more difficult, than others—that is, they require more computational power, or more time to compute. By transforming a problem, we may reduce the strength necessary to solve it. And, indeed, my clients do something similar: They don't deal with raw data about their environment; they use transformed—simplified— data. That may help them function successfully, but it may not help me obtain the data behind their simplifications. Because we each lump the world in our own unique way,

**One person's help is another's hardship.**

Or, in more memorable terms,

**One person's lump is another person's lumps.**

I call this LUMP, for The Law of Unavoidably Messy Peculiarity, because it's a corollary of The Lump Law. Consultants are limited by LUMP and The Lump Law, but there's a way around these laws—one of the true secrets of consulting. To explain, I have to tell a story about my youth that will reveal more than I would like about just how ancient I am.

---

[1] Gerald M. Weinberg, *An Introduction to General Systems Thinking: Silver Anniversary Edition* (New York: Dorset House Publishing, 2001), p. 105.

## The First Law of Good Consulting

When I was in college, there were no electronic computers anywhere on campus—in fact, there were just three or four in the world. But there were *computers*—and I was one of them. The Physics department paid me 90 cents an hour to perform long, laborious, and tedious calculations using a pencil, some paper, and a bulky, loud mechanical Friden calculator. The Friden helped because it could do large multiplications in several seconds of clattering and clunking, rather than the minutes it would take me to do them with pencil and paper. Still, it took long enough that whenever I had to compute a formula with something like

$$B = 3 * A$$

I would translate it to a weaker form,

$$B = A + A + A$$

Even though this meant performing two additions instead of one multiplication, I could do these two additions faster than the Friden could do one multiplication.

Similarly, the formula,

$$B = A^3$$

would be weakened to

$$B = A * A * A$$

Two multiplications were much easier to perform than a single exponentiation, which, in fact, neither the Friden nor I could do at all without a table of logarithms.

Logarithms represent a single multiplication that can be reduced to the following steps:

- look up the logarithm of A
- look up the logarithm of B
- add the two logarithms
- look up the antilogarithm

When I was in high school, we were taught this rather formidable process because we had no calculators, not even Fridens. Fridens made multiplication almost as weak as addition, and nowadays, processing power has increased so much that calculators have made exponentiation as weak as multiplication and addition. Nobody teaches this logarithmic transformation, because even if I need exponentiation, I don't need logarithms—as long as I have a calculator, even one of those free calculators given away at the corner gas station or bank. Today's young whippersnappers don't realize how lucky they are! Even in my most maudlin nostalgic moments, I don't miss logarithms one bit.

Now that we have electronic calculators and computers, we don't need these particular strength-reducing transformations. But the human mind—my mind, certainly—remains rather fixed in its reasoning abilities. For some of us, pictures are much easier to comprehend than words, so transforming a set of numbers into a graph is a strength-reducing operation. Others, however, have never grasped graphs, but easily understand stories that contain essentially the same information. Some prefer the original numbers. Or a metaphor, picture, or formula. What's weak for some is strong for others.

When I'm getting information from lots of different people—as I usually do to establish context—I have to be equipped with a variety of potentially strength-reducing transformations:

- words to pictures of various kinds
- pictures to words
- numbers to metaphors
- metaphors to pictures
- graphs to stories
- stories to numbers
- words to three-dimensional physical models
- words to formulas
- concepts to examples
- examples to concepts
- formulas to pictures
- formulas to numbers
- numbers to pictures
- numbers to words
- words to actions or demonstrations
- actions to pictures
- actions to formulas
- and many, many others

These transformations are all part of my Fish-Eye Lens. I think of them as different filters. I'm prepared to use whichever filter—whichever strength-reducing translation—allows my clients to use the mental form they prefer. And, I also come prepared to test for what's easiest by fitting my Fish-Eye Lens with one filter, then another.

Switching filters requires discipline. Remember The Law of the Hammer? It reminds me to test different filters:

**The child who receives a hammer for Christmas will discover that everything needs pounding.**[2]

Any photographer can tell you that hammering is not likely to improve a filter, yet sometimes when I'm frustrated with trying to understand a client, I start hammering away, using one and only one of my filters. This is The First Law of Bad Management, or, if you like, The First Law of Bad Consulting:

**When something isn't working, do more of it.**[3]

My Fish-Eye Lens, with its case full of filters, helps me remember not to be a bad consultant—at least not this kind of bad consultant. Instead, I use The First Law of Good Consulting:

**When something isn't working, do something else.**

You may recognize this as the source of Marvin's Fourth Great Secret, which we saw in Chapter 4:

**Whatever the client is doing, advise something else.**[4]

## Don's Deviance Derivation

I'm often fooled when listening to clients give "raw data" that are actually lumped in some way. My colleague and two-time coauthor Don Gause designed an exercise that taught me one way to notice smoothed data: When speaking to a large audience, Don asks people to pick random numbers from 1 to 100. When he tabulates their choices, he invariably finds a scarcity of numbers ending in 0 or 5. Obviously, their

---

[2] Gerald M. Weinberg, *The Secrets of Consulting* (New York: Dorset House Publishing, 1985), p. 53.
[3] Gerald M. Weinberg, *Quality Software Management, Vol. 1: Systems Thinking* (New York: Dorset House Publishing, 1992), p. 62.
[4] *The Secrets of Consulting*, pp. 7, 41.

picks were not random at all—but influenced by their bias that "round" numbers are not random.

The members of the audience probably know that if all the figures on your tax form end in zero, the tax auditors will notice and think the numbers have been fabricated—since round numbers "can't be random." But out of millions of tax returns, some of them, at random, ought to have quite a few numbers ending in zero.

I've heard that when an expedition measured the height of Mt. Everest, they got the figure of 29,000 feet. Since that would have looked like an approximation, they changed the figure to 29,002 feet—less accurate, but more believable.

In other words, the world isn't (usually) that neat, so when trying to see the environment, I use Don's Deviance Derivation:

**If it's too regular, it's not an observation; it's a formulation.**

There's nothing wrong with smoothing the world—the way people perceive their world is an essential part of the total context I'm trying to see. But I may want to go beyond or behind their formulations to reveal the deviant data.

For example, on an assignment for a client suffering from security breaches, I received the following assurance from the security director, Forrie: "Everybody here changes their password at least once a month." The word "everybody" was a bit too smooth for me, so I asked Forrie, "How do you know this?"

He seemed a bit offended by this question but went on to explain, as if to a young child: "Well, I suppose you wouldn't know this, but if your password hasn't changed within the past month, the system won't let you in until you choose a new one. Everybody *here* knows that."

"Oh, sorry. But you can see why I wouldn't know," I said. That satisfied Forrie, but didn't satisfy me. Here, according to Don's Deviance Derivation, was big-time lumping, and I was going to check it out.

I interviewed five employees about how they handled the lockouts. One said he kept two passwords and alternated them each month. A second said he had twelve passwords—he just used the name of whatever month it was. The other three all used the same system: They changed their password to something simple, then immediately changed it back to the familiar value they always used.

Forrie was not pleased to receive data that contradicted his simple formulation, and he wanted me to name my five informants. I asked him why he wanted to know, and he snapped, "So I can get their managers to order them to *really* change their passwords every month!"

Forrie's formulation went much deeper than I originally estimated. He apparently believed that people are messily peculiar but not so peculiar that they couldn't be forced by mechanical means to do something that was structured but very inconvenient. Moreover, he believed that managers could force people to use the system properly—even though the only way managers could enforce the password rule was to know their employees' passwords, thus defeating the whole point of the system. Finally, he believed that somehow the five people I interviewed just happened to be the *only* five who didn't really change their passwords every month.

All in all, Forrie taught me a lot about the context of his organization, as well as about the way security directors formulate the world. Of course, I suppose not *all* security directors think like Forrie. Is that possible?

## Separation (or Not) of Variables

Lumping is just one way my clients become "messily peculiar" by trying to simplify their environment. Perhaps the second most popular simplification technique is just the opposite of lumping—splitting one thing into two or more relatively independent parts. Scientists call this process "separation of variables."

For example, let us assume that whenever we have a population of a million bacilli in a patient's lung, one mutant bacillus will be resistant to streptomycin (S) and one to isoniazid (I). If the patient is given drug S, all the bacilli are killed except for the one S-resistant mutant. This multiplies, and eventually we have a new population of a million S-resistant organisms. Among these may be a random mutant that is also I-resistant, and if we now change to drug I, we may soon find that the patient is infected with doubly resistant bacilli. On the other hand, if we attack with both S and I, we reduce the probability of a spontaneously occurring, doubly resistant mutant to one in a million million.[5]

In other words, to understand how to defeat the bacilli, the scientists break down the lump called "bacilli" into two lumps, S and I. Then they hit these tiny critters with two drugs lumped together, to prevent them from separating variables. In effect, they impose The Law of Unavoidably Messy Peculiarity on the poor bacilli, which get wiped out. The scientist's help is the bacilli's hardship.

[5] For more on the fight against viruses, see M. Burnet and D.O. White, *Natural History of Infectious Disease* (London: Cambridge University Press, 1972), p. 220.

Now, if I want to create a difficult problem for someone (like a hacker trying to break into a computer system), it helps to know how the brain solves problems. I can create a difficult problem by *preventing a separation of variables*. Against hacking, for example, I can create a set of locks, all of which must be broken at once in order to enter the system. My clients do this unconsciously, not (I hope) to make my job difficult, but to make theirs easy. But it makes my job difficult all the same, and sometimes it feels as if they are intentionally "locking" their environment from my prying eyes.

I use my Fish-Eye Lens to remind me of the tools I have for understanding the context, many of which I presented in *The Secrets of Consulting*. Looking at them now, it's easy to see how many of them are ways of separating variables. For example, there's Sparks's Law of Problem Solution:

**The chances of solving a problem decline the closer you get to finding out who was the cause of the problem.**[6]

Like a prism diffracting white light into a variety of colors, Sparks's Law helps me separate two variables the client has combined. In the particular case that taught me Sparks's Law, the problem itself had been lumped with the problem of who was to be blamed for the problem. Notice, too, that if I need to use Sparks repeatedly, I may have discovered something else about the context—that this organization is deeply immersed in the habit of blaming.

Other guidelines from *The Secrets of Consulting* have also helped me separate variables. For example, I admonish myself to "Deal gently with systems that should be able to cure themselves."[7] This reminds me to separate diagnosis from cure, being sure to do the one before even considering the other.

Another example that applies directly to understanding the context is, "Look for what you like in the present situation, and comment on it."[8] This reminds me that clients often lump all the good aspects of the context with the bad, and then the good get lost to their view—and to mine. By commenting on what's good, I help my clients (and myself) separate variables in a new way.

---

[6] *The Secrets of Consulting*, p. 58.
[7] *The Secrets of Consulting*, p. 39.
[8] *The Secrets of Consulting*, p. 59.

This brings me to those cases in which the clients present me with variables already separated—possibly for their convenience, but usually for mine. For instance, clients think they are being helpful when they classify everyone as either friend and foe, a separation of variables that may not be contributing to solving their problems.

## The Background Blindfold

Since all these tools are available to my clients, too, why is seeing what MacKenzie calls the Giant Hairball such a problem? Why don't they just look around them? One reason is that the context is always there, always impinging on their senses. The context becomes invisible because of the psychological phenomenon of *habituation*—the successive reduction of response to a repetitive stimulus. In common parlance, this is called The Background Blindfold:

**The fish is always the last to see the water.**

Habituation is a way of canceling out constant stimuli in the environment, and it probably occurs in almost all complex systems. Otherwise, the systems would be overloaded with sensory data that most of the time don't carry much information. Habituation is a way of lumping the constants into a category of "things that I don't need to pay attention to because they're always there."

When something new first appears in our environment, we're very stimulated. But after it remains for a while and seems to hold neither threat nor opportunity, we (unconsciously) make it part of our model of the constant environment. It has become habituated out of our awareness, and now its *removal* will excite our interest.

A stunning example of the removal of a habituated stimulus is shown in Satyajit Ray's film *The World of Apu*.[9] When Apu gets the news of his wife's death, he throws himself onto his bed and remains unable to move for days. Ray shows Apu lying in bed in this state until suddenly his alarm clock *stops* ticking. Apu is startled out of his lethargy and starts on the road to recovery, but the real impact is on the viewer, who had also become habituated to the ticking of the clock. Of course, the viewer is utterly unaware of the ticking until it stops—and the silence strikes like a thunderbolt.

Similarly, my clients are habituated to the context in which they spend their working days, and they generally notice it only when it

---

[9] *The World of Apu*, 117 min., Satyajit Ray Productions, India, 1959.

changes. Therefore, they are not naturally good sources of information about their environment. They have habituated the context away; they are the fish, and it is their water.

### The Foreground Fantasy

Another kind of bias arises directly from The Background Blindfold. If people are habituated to the ordinary things in their environment, they are automatically biased toward noticing things that are *not* habitual. I call this The Foreground Fantasy:

**The fish is always the first to notice the air.**

Indeed, some exceptional event is often what triggers a call for a consultant—a system crashes, a project fails to produce a viable product, an employee (or two, or ten) quits, Chicken Little runs around crying that the sky is falling. Regardless of how real the threat is, Tom Crum's definition of FEAR as "Fantasy Experienced As Reality" takes effect, and everyone starts to flop around like fish out of water.[10] That's when they usually call me.

Fortunately, when I'm summoned as an external consultant, I'm truly a fish out of my usual water. My Fish-Eye Lens is the perfect tool for putting the background and foreground in perspective. Once I have this perspective, I can perhaps calm the excited ones and rouse the habituated ones.

### The Five-Minute Rule

Even when my clients become aware of some of their surroundings, they are subject to a variety of observational biases, as I am. Here's an example I recall involving *Time*'s Man of the Century, Albert Einstein:

> *Ernst Strauss, Einstein's assistant from 1944 to 1948, tells the story of searching for a paper clip with Einstein. They found a bent one, so they needed a tool to straighten it. When he found a box of new paper clips, Einstein took one out and bent it into a tool to straighten the other one. When Strauss pointed out how ridiculous this was, Einstein said, "Once I am set on a goal, it becomes difficult to deflect me."*

---

10 Tom F. Crum, *The Magic of Conflict* (New York: Touchstone, Simon & Schuster, 1987).

I love Einstein stories like this; they make me feel so smart. As a consultant, I'm generally called in when there's a problem, and generally that means that my clients, like Einstein, have become overly focused on a solution. Thus, they may fail to see relevant factors in their environment. Often, as in this story, they fail to see solutions they are holding in their hands.

That's where The Five-Minute Rule comes from. As I mentioned in Chapter 5, during my Wishing Wand consultation with Mel,

**Clients always know how to solve their problems, and always tell the solution in the first five  minutes.**[11]

Inexperienced consultants may have a hard time believing that this rule could be true. When they encounter a school of flopping fish, they're so overwhelmed with their own issues that they forget to focus their Fish-Eye Lens. They miss the solution that their clients, like Einstein, are holding but not seeing.

SATIR'S THREE UNIVERSAL QUESTIONS

How do I get all this information about the context, so I can strip out all these biases? As I do with my Mirror and my Telescope, I use my Fish-Eye Lens to answer Virginia Satir's Three Universal Questions, which I modify slightly to account for the entire organization and all its people:

- How did they get here? (Past)

- How do they feel about being here? (Present)

- What would they like to have happen? (Future)

Following are some examples of Big Picture questions that help me see the larger context and that once again make an enormous difference in how I approach an assignment.

*How Did They Get Here? (Past)*

To approach this first question, I call on Boulding's Backward Basis:

**Things are the way they are because they got that way.**[12]

---

[11] *The Secrets of Consulting*, p. 67.
[12] *The Secrets of Consulting*, p. 58.

My awareness of the evolution of the situation helps me understand it better. With this, I keep the following questions in mind:

- Can I get a history of the organization? Is it an official history, and if so, how does it differ from the unofficial oral history that I hear from people?

- What's the organization's past experience with consultants? What was the process by which I was chosen? Is that process typical in this organization?

- How long do people typically stay in this organization? How long do they stay in the same job? Where do they come from before they get here?

- Is this a profit-making company, and if so, what is its history of profitability? If it's a nonprofit, what is the vision that inspired its creation?

*How Do They Feel About Being Here? (Present)*

To approach the second question, I call on Brown's Brilliant Bequest:

**Words are often useful, but it always pays to listen to the music (especially your own internal music).**[13]

I can get the best impression of this part of the context by simply walking around and meeting people, being friendly and inquisitive about their work and the things I see around their workplaces. Of course, if the people who invited me discourage me from walking around and doing this, that tells me more than I could find out from days of strolling. I keep questions like these in mind:

- Are the people I meet eager? Happy? Friendly?

- Do they like their surroundings? What kind of evidence do I find in the way they organize their workspaces? Do they feel free to show evidence of their personal life, and if so, what do they show and not show?

---

[13] *The Secrets of Consulting*, p. 85.

- What evidence do they show of professionalism and of how they measure it? Do I see certificates as evidence of training, and if so, what training are they showing off? Do they keep things tidy? Do they keep things so tidy it looks as if they are afraid of citations for a disorderly workplace?

- Are people puzzled about what's expected of them in this organization? Do their titles have meaning? Do they use their titles, and if so, how do they use them? As badges of honor? As attempts to force respect?

- Are they sure of themselves? Do they feel empowered to make decisions and be backed up by the organization?

- Is this the right mood for succeeding in this job? If not, what would have to happen to get them in the right mood?

### What Would They Like to Have Happen? (Future)

This third question is often harder to get at, because each organization has official aspirations that seldom reveal what people are really hoping will happen. I keep the following questions in mind:

- Why did they look for a consultant? Was it for reassurance about what they've already decided? For the expertise? As a scapegoat? To hold their hands?

- How long do they want me here?

- How were people chosen to work with me on this assignment? Did they feel they had a choice, and if so, why did they choose? Why were they chosen? How many people wanted this assignment but were not chosen? Is that a typical method of selection?

- What will success look like to the organization? Can the team members give examples of previous efforts that were successful? Unsuccessful? Can they explain why the efforts were regarded that way?

- What do they fear? Do they seem to be hiding something from me? How do they react when I ask about what they're hiding?

THE FISHY-EYE LENS

I can overcome many of the biases that prevent my clients from seeing their own environment, but ultimately, I need to take my own pictures of the context. As I search for context information, I keep my Fish-Eye Lens hooked up with my *Fishy*-Eye Lens, a tool that senses things that smell fishy. This tool operates under what I call The Incongruence Insight:

> *A great turning point in my consulting life came when Nancy Brown, one of the world's great consultants, was observing me working with a client. I had just made a fantastic rational analysis of the client's problem, but it somehow felt all wrong. At a break, when I asked Nancy what I was missing, she said quietly, "Sometimes when I'm not getting anywhere with the words, I listen to the music." I wasn't exactly sure what she meant, but I resolved to try it after the break.*
>
> *The client told me that his relationship with his co-workers was a great problem, but his voice and posture had been so relaxed that when I compared the words and the "music," I saw that his words made no sense.  On the other hand, when my questions touched on his relationship with his boss, he started to fidget and his voice acquired a strained tone. Using this music as a clue, I quickly moved into an area I'd missed entirely, having been misled by his words which said, in effect, "Don't waste your time looking there." This led to a new definition of the problem as well as several new solution ideas.*
>
> *What is missing in these cases is* congruence *between the words being used and the emotions being expressed.  Over the years since that lesson, I've learned that the ability to sense incongruence is the consultant's most powerful "What's missing?" tool. I call this The Incongruence Insight:*
>
> **When words and music don't go together, they point to a missing element.**
>
> *The most effective method of finding that element is simply to comment on the incongruity and allow the client to respond.  All I said to this client was, "I notice that your hands tremble while you talk about your wonderful relationship with your boss." I didn't try to interpret this incongruence, but merely brought it to his conscious*

*attention. He looked startled for a moment, glanced down at his hands as if to confirm what I said, and then opened up to me about how he feared his boss so much that he was afraid to talk to anyone about it, lest there be repercussions.*[14]

Since I wrote *The Secrets of Consulting*, I've been gathering juicy examples of incongruent messages about the context in an organization. Following are some examples:

- A telecommunications company started a program of "outstanding contribution recognition." Each month, the winners were photographed receiving a plaque from a senior executive, and the photos were prominently displayed at the cafeteria entrance. In the text below each photograph, the outstanding contributor's name was given in plain 12-point type; the executive's was given in 18-point bold.

- A consulting company decided it needed to raise employee morale. The managers conducted an "anonymous" survey, but insisted that every employee write an identifying number on the survey form, "for control purposes."

- A related case was the manager who kept a bullwhip on the wall in his office. He said it was a souvenir from a leadership course he took, and it reminded him of the major lesson of that course—individual initiative.

I characterize these conflicts as "right-left messages." When right-hand messages (words) are contradicted by left-hand messages (actions), guess which ones will be heard—that is, which ones make up the real context of the organization.

There's a meta-context, too, in that most of these managers couldn't fathom the incongruity when it was pointed out to them. That *really* tells you something about the managerial context of these organizations.

But perhaps the managers were lying, and the incongruity was intentional. In that case, I can apply The Inverse Gilded Rule:

**If something's faked, it must need fixing.**[15]

To seek out right-left messages quickly, I ask about things like the organization's vision statements, company newsletters, and press releases. I

[14] *The Secrets of Consulting*, p. 84.
[15] *The Secrets of Consulting*, p. 49.

check for behavior that aligns with these public pronouncements—or doesn't. Then I ask about that. Either way, my Fishy-Eye Lens reveals important information about the context in which I will be working.

## THE CROOKED CHANNEL CLEANSER

The Fish-Eye Lens is a metaphor for the sensory channels through which I perceive the context in which I'm working, but whether these channels are physical or metaphorical, they must be kept clean. Let me give a funny example:

> *Up at our cabin in Pecos, New Mexico, we're connected to the world by one thin telephone line that runs through the mountains. A few years ago, we had a peculiar problem: Our phone kept dialing wrong numbers. We have several extensions, and all did the same thing, so I figured the problem wasn't the handset, but something further down the line.*
>
> *I tried to call for repair, but because the phone was misdialing, I kept getting directory assistance. I tried to tell the operator that my phone was misdialing, but she told me I'd have to call the repair department for repairs. After several cycles of misdialing and trying to explain to the operator what happened, I gave up and drove the Jeep down the mountain ten miles to the phone company where I could describe my problem face-to-face to Drew, the repair man who often came to our house when there was trouble.*
>
> *Drew, as usual, was friendly and helpful. But he was puzzled. "Why didn't you just call me on the repair number?" he asked. "You could have saved yourself the trip." He couldn't seem to grasp the concept that the communication system itself was adding error to the situation.*

I wasn't really surprised by Drew's reactions, because when something like this happens (often unnoticed) in personal interactions, people rarely grasp what is going on. I call this kind of mystery a Crooked Channel Conundrum. It's cleared up by applying The Crooked Channel Cleanser:

**When you're having trouble understanding what you're receiving, first check that your channel is congruent.**

In other words, I try to keep my Fish-Eye Lens polished; otherwise, I won't know if I'm seeing the world or merely seeing the distortions of the Lens. If I am straight with people, I can debug my crooked interactions with them—it's like providing a constant environment for debugging software, where *I* am the test environment itself.

Some environments are easier to keep clean and consistent than others. Just as it's easier to maintain an off-line test environment for computer systems, it's easiest for humans to communicate clearly in written correspondence. You have time to think things through and to remove as much incongruence as possible. The trade-off, though, is that you don't have the quick feedback on incongruence that you would have in a real-time interaction. E-mail gives you faster feedback, but sometimes it's too fast; on-line chats and face-to-face meetings are the hardest to keep clean.

In all environments, I do my best to be as congruent as possible. I try to ensure that what I see is not the result of my own incongruence, distorting what is really out there.

And that's why I need my Gyroscope, which I describe in the next chapter.

## *the gyroscope*

**Even if only one shoe doesn't fit, you limp.**
**—Anonymous**

$T$he Gyroscope represents my ability to be congruent, or balanced in my inner feelings and outer actions.[1] I need this balance in order to use all of my tools effectively. It has a special meaning for me, because as I mentioned earlier, my father gave me my first gyroscope. To this day, I remain fascinated by its ability to balance itself, and to restore its balance when disturbed. Sometimes, I think that The Gyroscope is too complex for my personal tool kit, but then I remember that restoring balance to my life *is* complex, and it is something that I must always try to do.

## LIFE BALANCE AND CONGRUENCE

One of the complications about balance is that there are two kinds: big balance (balance in your life) and little balance (congruent behavior in every interaction). Without big balance, you'll have a hard time staying congruent in each little balance situation. And without congruence in small things, you'll have a hard time moving toward a balanced life.

My tool kit symbol for big balance is The Oxygen Mask, because without balanced breathing, life ceases to exist. I discuss The Oxygen Mask in Chapter 15. For little balance, or congruent interactions, my symbol is The Gyroscope. In this chapter, I hint at some of the lessons contained in The Oxygen Mask chapter, and in that chapter, of course, I will refer to this one. Bear in mind, though, that life balance and congruence can only be separated in books.

## *Not a Place, but a Process*

If you watch a gyroscope in action, you'll soon become aware that its balance is not a thing, not a position, but a process. Its spinning gives it an alignment that, when disturbed, is restored because of the way physics works. Human congruence is analogous to the gyroscope's process. Your sense of self gives you an alignment that, when disturbed, is restored because of the way your mind works. Your inner feelings become aligned, or congruent, with your external behavior. Many disci-

---

[1] Some of the material in this chapter appears in *Quality Software Management, Vol. 3: Congruent Action* (New York: Dorset House Publishing, 1994), which has a much more extensive explanation of congruence and its applications.

plines involving real-time performance—music, martial arts, athletics, acting—speak of this process as "finding your center" or "centering."

Much of consulting is also real-time performance, so every consultant needs to learn a process of centering. To move toward congruence, you have to be able to feel where your center is, notice when you lose it, and quickly make choices that restore it. Here's how my cowgirl friend and colleague Sue Petersen explained centering to a group of software engineering managers:

> *I haven't taken judo or any of the martial arts, but I've learned centering from training animals and raising kids. I know I'm centered when something maddening happens and I can feel myself step back and choose my response instead of going from the gut and blowing it. It only takes a fraction of a second, and it's saved my life more than once. I can almost always do it with the kids, usually with the critters, and usually not with my dad or the in-laws.*

## Perfect Poise Paradox

With the kids, either you learn centering or you're driven crazy—and that's also true of consulting. In earlier chapters, I showed how my Mirror, my Telescope, and my Fish-Eye Lens help me understand the aspects of self, other, and context. Yet, it's hard to work effectively with *any* of these tools when I'm not able to get myself in balance. And why is it that so many consultants have trouble with centering? Whenever I write about centering, I get letters like this one:

> *It's all very nice to say that I ought to be centered in myself before I make big decisions, but whenever I get into some sort of negotiation, I lose track of myself, what I want, and what's good for me. What do you suggest?*

The first part of the question is easy. When I first notice that I'm starting to lose myself, I STOP whatever I'm doing. This is the "fraction of a second" that Sue describes. Then I concentrate on how I'm breathing, and I switch to a smooth, regular rhythm.

The rest follows, but sometimes people have trouble doing even this much:

*I've tried the breathing thing, and sometimes it works. But some-times it doesn't, like when another person is blasting at me in a loud voice. What should I do then?*

Centering is not magic. Sometimes it doesn't work—that is, it doesn't produce the result I so fervently desire at the moment. So, when I can't even get my breathing under control, I find a way to leave the situation. If I wish to continue, I come back later, when I've somehow managed to restore my balance. If I find myself *unable* to leave, then that's a sure sign I *must* leave, now—and not return to the situation. That is no situation for me.

I needed many years to learn how to center myself well, mostly because I was confusing congruence with perfection. As cowboy wisdom tells us,

**If you want to stay single, look for the perfect mate.**

In the same vein, we have The Perfect Poise Paradox:

**If you want to stay incongruent, try to be perfectly congruent.**

There are many ways to center yourself, but none of them are perfect. If you are convinced that perfection is necessary, or even possible, you are condemned to an endless, incongruent search for "the one right way."

## Internal Messages

So, instead of trying to beat The Perfect Poise Paradox, let's just look at some of the many tools for centering, tools that have worked for me.

We've already seen the problems that survival rules can cause, and this impossible quest for perfection is just one more example of how survival rules produce incongruence. These rules drive our emotional state *as if* our very survival were at stake, and therefore function as unconscious programs that control our behavior. Once under the control of a survival rule, we cannot make the conscious choices Sue described as crucial to her centering process.

Perhaps when we were younger, following these rules was the best we could do. Even as adults, survival rules may actually guard our lives, but in the typical consulting work, there are few truly life-or-death situations. It only *feels* that way.

I could try to detect the presence of my survival rules by studying the incongruent coping behaviors they engender, such as casting blame, placating people, responding with irrelevant behavior, loving or hating to extremes, or acting superreasonable and excessively logical.[2]  Unfortunately, by the time I'm behaving in one of these classically incongruent modes, I usually can't do anything about it.  Besides, since I'm usually unaware of my *own* incongruent coping, I need a more reliable signal. One such signal is found in self-talk, all the *internal messages* I give myself, especially those messages that come wrapped in a strong emotional package.[3]  For example, underlying the incongruent coping might be fear, and that fear may come from telling myself, "I might make a mistake."

By itself, the statement "I might make a mistake" doesn't necessarily lead to fear.  One reaction might be fear, but consider these other responses: sadness, as in, "Several people will be let down if that happens, and I want to please them."  Or the feeling might be anger, as in, "I don't want to waste any time doing this darned thing over."  Or indifference, as in, "Well, I've made lots of mistakes before, so it's no big deal." Or excitement, as in, "Wow, most of my best learning has come from mistakes, so this is going to be a great opportunity."

Your feelings in response to a message may vary from mine because we each carry different life experiences into the feeling process. When these experiences have been codified into a survival rule, the feelings are particularly strong—generally fearful—and seem to be out of conscious control.  For instance, fear may arise in response to an internal message such as, "I might make a mistake," when it conflicts with a codified survival rule such as, "I must always be perfect."

Without that survival rule, I wouldn't expect such a strong fear to arise, or the incongruent ways I would cope with that fear.  Instead, I would try to transform the internal message into something like, "I'll do my best to be congruent, but perfection isn't possible."

## The Parliament of Fears

Internal messages provide advance warning that I am about to behave incongruently.  By listening to my internal messages and transforming them in light of high self-esteem, I can thwart incongruent action before it happens.  This doesn't mean "stuffing my feelings," but as one of my

---

[2] *Quality Software Management, Vol. 3: Congruent Action*, pp. 26–41.

[3] For lots more on self-talk and how to change it, see Pamela E. Butler, *Talking to Yourself: Learning the Language of Self-Affirmation* (San Francisco: HarperSanFrancisco, 1991).

colleagues put it, "really remaking your internal landscape." Bertrand Russell, long ago, expressed this process in different language:

> The man who wishes to preserve sanity in a dangerous world should summon in his own mind a Parliament of fears, in which each in turn is voted absurd by all the others.[4]

Here are some examples of low self-esteem messages I've given myself in the course of my consulting work, the rules that may underlie them, and the way I reframed them into more congruent messages when my Gyroscope reminded me to notice my "Parliament of fears":

|  |  |
|---|---|
| *Incongruent:* | Someone will criticize my work. |
| *Underlying rule:* | I must always be above criticism. |
| *Congruent:* | Some criticism is inevitable; I take it as a gift. |
|  |  |
| *Incongruent:* | I might impose my ideas on my clients. |
| *Underlying rule:* | I must always stay out of other people's way. |
| *Congruent:* | Imposition goes with communication, to some degree. |
|  |  |
| *Incongruent:* | They will think I'm not a good consultant. |
| *Underlying rule:* | I must always make a good impression. |
| *Congruent:* | Even if someone thinks I'm no good, I can survive. |
|  |  |
| *Incongruent:* | They will think I'm not perfect. |
| *Underlying rule:* | I must always be perceived as perfect. |
| *Congruent:* | I'm not perfect, so I don't need to be seen as perfect. |
|  |  |
| *Incongruent:* | They might have a conflict over this. |
| *Underlying rule:* | I must always maintain harmony. |
| *Congruent:* | I don't need everyone to agree all the time. |
|  |  |
| *Incongruent:* | They might not like me if I don't agree. |
| *Underlying rule:* | I must always be liked by everyone. |
| *Congruent:* | I agree or disagree because I genuinely do. |

---

[4] Bertrand Russell, "Nightmares," *The Collected Stories of Bertrand Russell* (London: Allen & Unwin, 1972).

| *Incongruent:* | I should pretend it's important. |
| *Underlying rule:* | I must always take everything seriously. |
| *Congruent:* | I work with real problems in a real way. |

| *Incongruent:* | I might have to change (but I won't unless I'm forced). |
| *Underlying rule:* | I must always remain as my parents taught me to be. |
| *Congruent:* | I'm able to change if I want to. |

## The Body-Brain Behest

If I'm unaware that I'm acting incongruently, that is, in conflict with my inner feelings, I can hardly start a process of recovery. That's why the first step in recovering congruence is to notice my own incongruence. For me, the easiest way to do this is to listen to my internal messages, but there are other ways.

I often notice incongruence when I feel it in my body. My breathing may become shallow, rapid, or irregular. My posture may become rigid or unsteady, or I may find myself straining to keep my balance. Pain anywhere in my body is a reliable clue to incongruence—whether the pain is a cause or an effect. Or, I may be experiencing nausea, dizziness, or trembling—all reliable signs of incongruence.

Why are these signs reliable? Well, my body senses the real world, while my brain merely interprets the sensations the body provides. So, thoughts are secondary information and not as reliable. That's why I follow what I call The Body-Brain Behest:

**Trust your body, then your brain.**

## Parson's Peculiarity Principle

Listening to my body did not come naturally to me, because, like many American kids, I was taught that it wasn't nice to pay so much attention to my own problems, physical or otherwise. I had to practice consciously to tune into my body, so I suspect that many of my readers will not immediately be able to rely on such physical cues.[5] I was also taught

---

[5] There are a number of ways you can begin to sharpen your awareness of being physically off center. I found Tom Crum's "Magic of Conflict" workshops extremely helpful, along with his book *The Magic of Conflict* (New York: Touchstone, Simon & Schuster, 1987). Both the book and the workshops are based on the art of aikido.

to be logical, but logic isn't a very reliable incongruence detector—because incongruence is largely based on "facts not in evidence" rather than a reaction to the here-and-now situation.

A clue I find more helpful than direct logic is the awareness of illogic—that others are reacting to me in surprising ways, ways that do not seem to follow from the logic of the situation. That's because if I'm acting incongruently, I'm likely to trigger incongruent reactions in others.

Rather than blame others for incongruence, I ask myself, "What could I be doing to contribute to their behavior?" In other words, I use my Telescope and my Mirror together, as a Telescope/Mirror, to study the other person and myself. Here's how it worked for Parson, one of my consulting students:

> *I was telling one of the project managers that I'd like to see a plan to get her project back on schedule. As she handed me a folder containing her revised project plan, I became aware that the papers in her hand were rattling. That caught my attention, and I thought, how strange that the papers should rattle like that. Looking for an explanation, I noticed she was trembling, that her face was ashen, and finally that her eyes were wet.*
>
> *My first thought was "Oh, she's sick!" but then I remembered The Telescope/Mirror idea from class that she might be reacting to me. That seemed ridiculous, as I was merely talking to her normally, but I decided to check it out.*
>
> *The first thing I noticed about myself was that I was gripping the edge of my desk as if it were a safety rail between me and the Grand Canyon. I thought I should loosen the grip, but then I realized I would probably fall on my face toward her if I did. All this while I continued talking to her about the project plan, until I noticed that I was actually shouting and banging my other fist on the desk. That's when I had my big AHA!*

To help you remember to consider the true source of illogical behavior, I've coined Parson's Peculiarity Principle:

**If they're acting peculiarly, maybe they're reacting to something peculiar; maybe it's me.**

MAKING ADJUSTMENTS

Incongruence is stereotyped behavior. That's why it destroys effective consulting, which depends on original thinking. Fortunately, amazingly small changes can be used to disrupt the lockstep pattern of stereotyping. Once I've noticed some signs of incongruence, my next move is to start a series of minuscule adjustments.

For instance, Parson thought he should loosen his grip, but realizing he would fall, he first altered his posture to bring himself into a more centered position. Postural changes are often the first small adjustment, such as,

- standing up if sitting

- sitting down if standing

- moving if rigid

- stopping if moving

- getting both feet on the floor with my weight balanced

- flexing my legs at the knees a bit

With the first small change, the stereotype may begin to collapse in a cascade of other tiny adjustments. Changing my posture may make me aware of how tense I am, so the next thing I may want to do is relax. I can

- take control of my breathing

- stop clutching, pressing, or gripping

- relax any tense muscles

- slow down

- stop talking

Then, when I'm balanced and relaxed, I use my Heart to appreciate myself. Using my Mirror to see myself, I tell myself how well I've done to notice my incongruence and to make the small adjustments I've already accomplished. I need these messages of appreciation because if I don't respect myself, I cannot respect the other person. And if I don't respect the other person, I must ask myself, Why am I here?

*Making Contact with the Other Person*

Once I've made contact with myself, it's time for me to bring my Heart and Telescope into play to make contact with the other person or persons involved. In spite of what they may be saying, I pay close attention to their body signals, because those are a more reliable indicator than their words. When I do take in the words, I don't jump to my first interpretation—good or bad. Instead, I get verbal clarification. During the clarification process, I continue to watch their body signals. And mine.

Once I feel I have understood the other person, I can comment on the present situation from my point of view. I try to start my comments with the word "I," not "You" or "It." "You" sentences tend to sound like blaming; "It" sentences tend to sound too abstract or superreasonable. I also try to avoid using fake "I" sentences as a way of talking about the other person, such as,

| | |
|---|---|
| *Incongruent:* | You always make this same mistake. |
| *Disguised as:* | *I think that* you always make this same mistake. |
| *Better:* | I have a hard time recovering when you make this mistake. |

I try to stick to observations and avoid interpretations. To keep to the here-and-now, I use a present-tense verb. I avoid using vague, general-purpose nouns like "responsibility," "maturity," or "thoughtfulness":

| | |
|---|---|
| *Incongruent:* | You acted irresponsibly. |
| *Disguised as:* | *I feel that* responsibility is essential to optimal performance. |
| *Better:* | From what I have heard so far, I now believe that you acted irresponsibly when you <give specifics>. Am I misinterpreting something? |

This example, however, suggests another dangerous tendency of mine—becoming long-winded in an attempt to be clear. I remind myself: Keep it short—short words, short sentences, and not too many of them. I try to be as clear as possible, but rather than struggle or repeat, I try something like this:

| | |
|---|---|
| *Better:* | I'm feeling so emotional about this, I'm having a hard time speaking clearly. Am I being clear? |

Again, my Heart reminds me that if I can't be respectful of the other person, I shouldn't even try to make contact. I break it off and come back when it's a better time. I do the same for any other reason I can't make contact the way I'd like. Even if the other person doesn't think so, it's always okay to say,

> *Better:*    I'm having trouble saying how I feel right now. Let's do this later.

## Waiting for the Other Person to Respond

If I am able to stay involved with the interaction, I need to watch out for my tendency to become excessively intense, which may intimidate the other person. I've learned that the best way to control my intensity is to make my statement and then *wait for the other person to respond.*

Sometimes, I have to visualize what I'm saying with a large period at the end, or perhaps a question mark. And I never, never ask more than one question at a time, as in,

> *Incongruent:*    I don't want to offend anyone.
> *Disguised as:*    Did you understand that? Was I clear? Is it responsive to what you said? Would you like me to phrase it differently? I didn't hurt your feelings, did I? Am I talking too much? Are you having trouble getting a word in edgewise?

Nobody could respond congruently to this stream of placating questions, so I need to stop and breathe. I need to let the other person know by my eyes, posture, and tone of voice that I have reached a full stop. If the person is still not getting the message, I say, "I'm done." Then I stop.

I make one exception to the rule about not repeating myself. I do repeat the entire process as often as needed to reach congruence—or I leave for the time being. I know it's time to leave and regroup when nothing changes from one repetition to the next.

Even if the interaction doesn't work out well, I can always learn from it, using my Wisdom Box. Afterward, I sit down in a quiet place, take out my Magnifying Glass, put on my Detective Hat, and reflect on what I did and didn't do—not blaming, but emphasizing what I did well. This is how I learn to be more congruent, more of the time—one interaction at a time.

At the time of this writing, I've been consulting for almost a half-century, so I've had a lot of these incongruent interactions to practice on. Perhaps I've smoothed off some of the rough edges in my centering process, and although this may be good for my consulting business, it's often harmful to my coaching business. Without some of the rough edges to reveal what's going on inside of me, some of my students fall into The Perfect Poise Paradox. They think, "Jerry is perfectly congruent, so I should be, too." I hope I've managed to show that nothing could be further from the truth, for me or for them. Congruence is difficult and perpetual work—work that requires the use of every tool in my kit.

## What Congruence Means to a Consultant

Is congruence really worth all this hard work? Incongruence tends to be reflected in stereotyped, repetitive behavior. Congruence, however, is reflected in the ability to choose among many different external behaviors. Which style do you think is more valuable to your work as a consultant?

Self-worth is at the base of congruence and gives me permission to take risks—the risks required to be an effective consultant. Most especially, self-worth gives me permission to risk behaving in a way that *matches the way I feel inside*—hence the term *congruent*. Congruence doesn't mean that I act according to some script, not even my own script. It means that if I feel X (where X is angry, happy, sad, grateful, hurt, proud, or some other emotion), the following takes place:

- I say I feel X.

- I sound like I feel X.

- I look like I feel X.

- My whole body is congruent with X.

- I share my X feeling with you. Then, I can ask for help, if I choose to, but I know I will survive if I don't get the help I ask for.

The only way to always be at your best is to be mediocre. If you're trying for high quality, sometimes you won't feel up to it. But, as Sammy Davis, Jr., said, "A professional is one who does a good job even when he doesn't feel like it." Notice that he said "good," not "best" or "excellent" or "perfect" or even "very good."

That's what congruence means: I feel good enough about myself, even when I feel rotten, to tell you how I feel. That means I can use all of the tools in my kit, and so I have an excellent chance to be a professional consultant.

## CHALLENGES TO CONGRUENCE

Like any other tool, The Gyroscope presents its challenges. We've already seen the first—The Perfect Poise Paradox—a reminder that I can never achieve perfect congruence, whatever that means. But even when I manage to be congruent, more challenges lie in wait.

### Win, Lose, or Learn

For one thing, congruence allows me to speak up in situations in which incongruence would render me mute with emotion. In negotiations, for instance, I'm more likely to use my Wishing Wand and ask for what I want. But asking for what I want doesn't mean *getting* what I want, so in that sense, congruence doesn't necessarily work.

In the real world, congruence is generally the best posture to take, but the best isn't always good enough. There are *no* situations in which congruence *always* works, and that creates challenges:

- It challenges me by offering an excuse for my incongruent behavior. "Well, since congruence didn't work, I had to try something else, so I attacked him."

- It challenges my belief in congruence, offering me an easy excuse not to continue practicing my centering behavior.

- It challenges me by offering something to blame when I don't get what I want. I can say, "Well, I was congruent, but congruence doesn't always work, so what else could I do?" Of course, I may not have been congruent in the first place, but with this excuse, I won't have to look at my actions, so having something to blame challenges my learning, too.

But there's one sense in which congruence *does* always work (when I let it): Congruence always serves my Detective Hat and my Magnifying Glass, because congruence does assure that the information I get is reliable and not contaminated with my own incongruent baggage. For instance, if I congruently ask for what I want and don't get it, I do get information about the other people involved. But if I ask in a blaming way, I don't know whether or not their refusal was simply a reaction to my blaming.

So, as Virginia Satir was fond of saying,

**If you're congruent, you might win, or you might lose, but you can always learn.**

I call this Satir's Win/Lose/Learn Principle.

### The Qualified-but-Quiet Quandary

I became aware of another challenge as I began to improve my congruence batting average: I had observed that I always seemed to spend the most time working on the one problem I didn't know how to solve. The more congruent I was, the less often I got stuck. For one thing, I knew how to say, "I'm stuck on this one," and move on. Or, I'd say, "I'm stuck on this one. Can you help me?"

The less I got stuck, though, the more I was perceived as a powerful consultant who always seemed to have a ready answer for every problem. People were invoking the common, but incorrect, Mana Model:

**Certain people have big magic (mana) and certain people don't.**[6]

The more I was perceived as a powerful consultant with big magic, the more likely it was for my remarks to get magnified out of proportion. Sometimes, my offhand speculations were mistaken as commands to action. As I became a better consultant, I had to raise my reaction threshold—to keep quiet more often or speak up less. Therefore, the more influential you become as a consultant, the more you need to be sensitive to precisely what's going on inside yourself. Hence, The Qualified-but-Quiet Quandary:

**The more congruent you become, the more you have to watch what you say.**

---

[6] *Quality Software Management, Vol. 3: Congruent Action,* pp. 16, 308.

The only compensation for this quandary is that the more congruent you become, the easier it is to watch what you say.

### Starr's Surrogate Syndrome

Still more challenges emerge as you succeed at being congruent more of the time. My friend Dan Starr put it this way after returning from one of the advanced workshops my firm offers, the Organizational Change Shop:

> One of the things Change Shop didn't tell us about congruent communication is that if you get to be even fair-to-middlin' at it, other people start asking you to do it for them! They sort of say, "I notice you can tell so-and-so something that he/she really doesn't want to hear, and he/she doesn't get upset about it. I know that if I said that, there'd be a big fight, so can you deliver this message?"
>
> I suppose that's a start, in that at least people are observing that healthier communication is possible, but what I really want them to do is say, "I notice you can tell so-and-so something that he/she really doesn't want to hear, and he/she doesn't get upset about it. I know that if I said that, there'd be a big fight, so can you show me how to do that?" (Isn't that interesting? When I phrase the problem that way, I know what I have to do to get what I want. . . .)[7]

Dan's letter made me aware of something I took for granted: the way people notice your new behavior and ask you to be congruent *for them*. So, in Dan's honor, I call this Starr's Surrogate Syndrome:

**No matter how much you or they would like it, you can't be congruent for someone else.**

In my consulting, I frequently get requests to be the "congruence surrogate" for my clients, and I handle it in various ways. I agree with Dan that my goal should be to show my client how to do it, so the people involved can learn to be congruent, too, but that may be too much all at once. You don't start your consulting career by solving the conflicts in the Middle East, so don't start your congruence career with the toughest situation you can imagine.

Sometimes, I agree to act alone as the client's surrogate, so my client can observe that *someone* can actually handle what appears to be

---

[7] Dan Starr, personal communication, 1992. See *Quality Software Management, Vol. 3: Congruent Action*, p. 65.

an impossible situation. But doing so is likely to reinforce my client's belief in The Mana Model. More likely, I'll tell them that I'll do it, but only if they're present to watch, listen, and learn. Or, I'll coach and encourage the client—even if that's not what I was originally asked to do. I make the choice of actions depending on the extent of the client's progress toward more frequent congruence.

*Knaomi's Knowledge Knockout*

Upon reading some of the material in this chapter, my colleague Naomi Karten, an author herself, commented:

> *I can relate to everything and understand it intellectually, but would have a difficult time applying it after reading it. That is, I would need to practice it in a workshop type of setting to fully "get" it and internalize it. In written form, it's too easy to just gloss over. I can already relate to much of this from my own background and work, but I wonder about people coming to it for the first time.*

I share Naomi's worry. Starr's Surrogate Syndrome says nobody can be congruent for somebody else. When it comes to congruence, Knaomi's Knowledge Knockout says,

> **Experience is not just the best teacher, it's the only teacher.**

But that's not all, because lots of people have experience trying to be congruent but don't seem to get anywhere. That's because

> **Experience may be the only teacher, but it doesn't neces- sarily teach anything.**

What I learned from my experiences is that I had to find ways to practice congruence in a safe, receptive, helpful setting. Workshops are ideal, which is why I'm in the workshop business. But I've also learned lots by practicing with Dani, or with a group of three or more like-minded friends. Remember, it takes big balance to learn small balance.

# 13

## the egg,
## the carabiner,
## and the feather

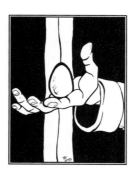

I have never let my schooling
interfere with my education.
—Mark Twain

In this chapter, I present three other tools that I've added to Virginia Satir's self-esteem tool kit: The Egg, The Carabiner, and The Feather. Each of these tools represents a different aspect of exploration, for me.

THE EGG

> **It is never too late to give up your prejudices.**
> **—Henry David Thoreau**

The Egg represents my ability to grow, develop, and learn, using all the parts of myself I need. Although I like to collect eggs—beautiful stone ones, usually—I'm actually allergic to the chicken kind. Perhaps this allergy explains why I took so long to associate The Egg with Virginia Satir's Seed Model—the concept that each of us comes into the world with all the tools we need to be complete human beings. When I'm stuck, my Egg reminds me that I have many tools that I don't realize I have, and that I also possess the ability to choose or make my own new tools. This chapter offers three examples of such additions to my original tool kit—The Carabiner, The Feather, and The Egg itself.

Virginia didn't have an Egg in her tool kit, but a little technique she often used as a Golden Key inspired me to add it to mine. One day, while Virginia, Dani, and I were starting to plan what ultimately became our Organizational Change Shop, I showed up late for a meeting. By way of apology, I muttered, "I'm not very good at time management. . . ."

". . . up until now," Virginia added. Hearing this, I was instantly transformed!

I had often watched this three-word intervention work its magic on other people, but this was the first time I experienced it myself. In a single instant, I was transformed from an immovable object resisting change to an irresistible force favoring change. I didn't have to accept a label given to me when I was small ("not very good at time management"), and I owned everything I needed to invalidate the label for myself, by myself. As we saw in Chapter 3, constant comments can be unlocked by those three words, the way they were transformed by the Nebraskan farmer on his one-hundredth birthday.

Up until now! Those three little Golden Key words were sufficient to open the door to the possibility of growth. Up until now, I had been, in my colleague Charlie Seashore's words, "in grave danger of growing." Oh, sure, I believed in growth—I was in the growth business, after all—but *not in the area of time management.* Somewhere along the way, someone had programmed my mind with the idea that poor time management was *an immutable part of my identity.*

The Egg reminds me that I have everything I need to grow. It also reminds me that nothing is immutably programmed into my mind—except its *programmability.* The ability of my mind to program itself is a far greater ability than any particular programming.

Each of us has innumerable unknown programs hidden inside of us. They cannot be erased, but they can always be *supplemented* by new programs. That's where Virginia's Principle of Addition comes from.[1] I don't try to subtract my poor time-management programs; instead, I add some better time-management programs that I can call upon when that ability is important to me. When it's not important, I can still call upon my old time-management programs, poor as they are. As my Egg reminds me, the choice is always mine.

Virginia Satir taught self-esteem to many people, but she was often discouraged by the many people who came to her to draw their esteem from her rather than to create their own, using their own tools. We were all sad when she died, but those who depended on her for their self-esteem were devastated. It's never a good idea to keep all your eggs in one basket—especially your self-esteem eggs and especially if it's someone else's basket. Even if that person is Virginia Satir, or even worse, me.

So, rather than make you dependent on me—or on Virginia, or on this book—for your supply of self-esteem tools, I offer you The Egg. Using your Egg, you can grow your own tools. I'm going to show you how I happened to grow a few tools that Virginia didn't give me, and then I'll invite you to grow your own.

The process of creating new tools is similar to any other change process. You start by centering yourself, using your Gyroscope. Then you make a connection with yourself, using your Mirror to show where you are "up until now" and using your Wishing Wand and Wisdom Box to let you know where you want to be. Which forgotten power do you want help remembering?

---

[1] Gerald M. Weinberg, *Quality Software Management, Vol. 3: Congruent Action* (New York: Dorset House Publishing, 1994), p. 161.

Then, with Courage Stick in hand, you move from past to present, using your Golden Key to know what's possible and your Detective Hat to figure out how to get it. If you have any problems, add one Egg to the recipe, to supply some creative, transforming idea that completes the metaphor for the tool. Last, what remains is to use your Courage Stick to practice, practice, practice—and voilà! A new tool.

## THE CARABINER

> **When you come to a fork in the road, take it.**
> **—Yogi Berra**

The Carabiner represents my ability to ensure my safety, to not take unnecessary risks, so I *can* take risks like the fork in the road at all. For those of you who don't climb mountains, the carabiner is a metal loop that attaches climbing ropes to pitons, the hooks that climbers embed in a cliff face. Carabiners protect the climbers from the dangers of falling. My colleague Linda Swirczek, who was an avid climber, gave me The Carabiner for my self-esteem tool kit. It gives me that moment to double-check my actions, so I can move ahead with the confidence the situation requires.

### Creativity and Freedom from Fear

In order to create new tools, I need all of my creativity, but fear reduces creativity. On the other hand, creativity reduces fear, because when I feel creative, I know I can construct a solution to any problem. Fear and creativity together form a positive feedback loop that tends toward runaway, but the direction it runs to—paralysis or freedom—can be determined by very tiny changes in the initial conditions of this chaotic system. The initial state of instability gives the change artist a lot of leverage at the beginning of something new—and The Carabiner is really helpful in reducing the initial fear.

Naturally, fear isn't the only factor in creativity, for there are many people who seem afraid of nothing but aren't very creative. Fear is one of the *brakes* on creativity. This positive feedback loop functions regardless of the source of the fear—and there are many potential sources, most of which arise from survival rules that can be reprogrammed. For example,

- Fear of *error* is one of the greatest killers of creativity, and generally arises from some sort of *perfection rule*. (For example, "I must always be, or appear to be, perfect.")

- *Personal pressure to succeed* creates fear, and above a certain point destroys thinking. (For example, "I must always succeed at everything I do.")

- Fear of *recognition,* paradoxically, can also be paralyzing. (For example, "I must never call attention to myself.")

- *The need to please others* can easily create conformity. (For example, "I must always please everybody.")

I'm often asked to facilitate groups whose main purpose is to enhance the creativity of the members. If the members are always trying to please each other, the coercive power of the group suppresses the creative power of its members. This situation matches the underlying paradox I find in many organizations. For instance, you can use coercive power to build a business, but a business cannot be built beyond a certain point without creative power.

Using all the technology in my self-esteem tool kit, I'm sometimes able to help these groups break this cycle of creativity depressed by fear. To do so, however, I have to battle a formidable double bind.

### The Magic Double Bind

Arthur C. Clarke, the science fiction writer, proposed the following law, called Clarke's Third Law:

**Any sufficiently advanced technology is indistinguishable from magic.**[2]

In my career, I have at times run a successful project, built a high-performing team, or conducted a stunning class. Each time, though, my technology seemed like magic to me, because I didn't really know how I did it. I do like to succeed, so perhaps I should be content with success alone. But I'm always afraid of not understanding my technology:

**If it's indistinguishable from magic, how do I know it won't go away next time?**

When I'm apprehensive, of course, I'm reluctant to change anything, no matter how small, for fear that the magic will flee. I feel trapped between the fear of losing the magic by change and the fear of losing the

---

[2] Arthur C. Clarke, *Profiles of the Future: An Inquiry into the Limits of the Possible* (New York: HarperCollins, 1973).

magic by *failing* to change—a classic example of the trap known as a "double bind" (you're damned if you do, damned if you don't).

Double binds tend to produce *paralysis* or *ritualized behavior*. For example, I'm often called upon to improve meetings, but I often find it difficult to persuade my clients to change anything. I've heard all sorts of reasons for not changing a meeting ritual, all of them arising from the double bind: "If we move to another room, it might not be as good as this one." "If we don't invite Jack to the next meeting, we might miss something he knows." "If we change the order of the agenda, we might not get through on time." "If we vote in a different way, we might make a poor decision." "If we don't order our doughnuts from Sally's Bakery, we won't have a successful meeting."

## Breaking the Bind

I'd find this behavior even more frustrating if I hadn't experienced the same double bind myself—for example, when my firm's faculty considers improvements to one of our workshops, Problem Solving Leadership (PSL). Over the years, lots of people have experienced what they call "the magic of PSL," and we're proud of that. But each time we consider a change, someone raises the fear that the change might make the magic disappear. Fortunately, each time this happens, someone is able to create a Carabiner by proving that the magic is not tied to the factor under consideration.

For instance, we've worried about changing the *hotel or city* where PSL is held. We do attempt to find magical sites, but then we remember that many PSLs have transformed mundane hotels in mundane cities into magical sites. This proves to us that the magic surely doesn't reside in the site, making it safe to move in that direction, thus freeing us from the double bind.

Or, we've worried about changing the *faculty* that teaches PSL. We certainly don't choose faculty members at random—each one is selected for his or her unique skills—but *every* faculty member has led many, many magical PSLs. So, the magic surely doesn't reside in any particular faculty member.

Or, we've worried about the *combination* of faculty members. We don't choose our co-training pairs at random, either, but all combinations experience magic. So, the magic surely doesn't reside in the faculty combination.

We've also worried about the *course materials* we use. We certainly don't choose materials at random, but we do change materials from class to class. In fact, no single course document has been used in every PSL, from the very first (back in 1974) to the most recent. So, the magic surely doesn't reside in particular materials, either.

I use this Carabiner approach to break my clients' double binds, pitting a counterexample as a Carabiner against each objection, each place we might fall or fail:

- *"If we move to another room, it might not be as good as this one."* "Ah, but remember when they were painting this room and we met downstairs? We had a good meeting then."

- *"If we don't use Microsoft Project, this project might fail."* "Could be, but we used other tracking software on project X, and we did a fine job."

- *"If we change to a new version of the operating system, we might have crashes."* "True. But we had a few crashes the last time we upgraded, and though it was some trouble, we dealt with them."

- *"If I clean up that code, the system might fail."* "That could happen, but the previous three times we cleaned up some code, we caught all the failures in our regression testing. So let's do it, but let's be careful."

## The Effective Use of Failure

Of course, I can't always produce a counterexample. In those cases, I try to demystify the magic and understand its underlying structure. To do this, I need examples where the magic didn't happen. In social engineering, as in all engineering, failures teach more than successes.

For instance, the PSL faculty became more aware of the source of PSL magic by observing a few times that the magic *didn't* "work." Usually, people come to PSL voluntarily, but not always. Once in a while, someone is *forced* to come to PSL to be "fixed," but people who have been labeled as "broken" may resent the whole experience and may not feel much PSL magic at all.

From these rare failures of PSL magic, we have identified one key magical component, The Choice Charm:

**People are there because they have *chosen* to be there.**

Curiously, the same component works in creating magical meetings, magical projects, and magical teams. When people are given a choice, they *are* the magic. Or, more precisely, they *create* the magic.

We open all our workshops, meetings, and projects by telling people, "Feel free to drop out and observe, or to argue with us if you don't agree." And then we reinforce this Carabiner principle at every opportunity.

When people *choose* to attend a workshop, to participate in a project, or to join a team, they feel safe to plunge themselves fully and creatively into the experience, rather than simply going through the motions. Consultants can thus have a magic advantage over employees: They always know that they've *chosen* this assignment, so they can always throw themselves into it without reservation. And, if conditions change, they can always remove themselves without guilt or hesitation.

Employees can have this choice, too, but they often forget—just as some consultants forget and feel forced to take an assignment out of economic necessity. Then they become as cautious as a naked man climbing a barbed wire fence. When I notice this behavior, I know it's time to get out The Carabiner.

My own Carabiner reminds me of the connections among safety and choice and creativity each time I choose a new assignment. If I feel forced, I won't feel safe and I won't do my magical best. Without a Carabiner, I won't have access to all the magical tools that live inside of me.

THE FEATHER

> **Life is too important to be taken seriously.**
> **—Oscar Wilde**

Even with my Egg and my Carabiner, my creativity sometimes gets stuck and won't come out. That's why I added a Feather to my tool kit. My Feather gives me the ability to loosen up when I'm stuck, so I can use my other tools.

The Feather represents my ability to tickle myself and others, and not to take anything, including myself, too seriously. I added The Feather to my tool kit on Wednesday, February 24, 1988. I know the exact date because I kept the newspaper clipping that inspired me:

> *NEW YORK—A depressed young man unable to control a compulsion to keep washing his hands put a .22 caliber rifle in his mouth, pulled the trigger, and survived with his compulsion cured.*

*"His IQ did not change. There was no change personality-wise. He did not become an automaton. His symptoms are gone,"* said his doctor, [who] . . . describes the suicide attempt as "successful radical surgery."*

It so happens that on Wednesday, February 24, 1988, I was working with a client, trying to help a project team find a solution to a bet-your-company problem. We were stuck, seriously stuck. After a depressingly fruitless morning session, we broke for lunch. That's when I read the article.

After lunch, I read the article to the whole group. "So," I concluded, "we at least have a chance. One of you can shoot yourself in the head, and maybe that will give you a better idea than what we've come up with so far."

Someone said, "That's pretty drastic. How about just banging our heads on the wall until we come up with something?"

Another chimed in, "I'm going to hang out the window upside down. Maybe something good will drain down from my feet."

And, then, with a gaggle of giggles and a cask of cackles, we proceeded to brainstorm our way out of the impasse. By realizing that we could never control everything, and that even the most ridiculous suggestion may sometimes yield good results, we stopped taking ourselves so seriously and broke the snare of our sobriety.

### Felicity's Feather Philosophy

Some people seem to have been born with their Feather, never taking themselves too seriously. Felicity was one of them, or so I thought. I first met Felicity and her twin sister, Fanny, at a conference. At the time, they were both unemployed and hunting through the conference's job fair. Fanny seemed understandably morose, but Felicity was wearing a lighthearted smile. When I suggested that I might have some good contacts for them, Felicity told me about their work history:

> *Fanny and I have always been identical in almost every way. All through school, we dressed alike, took every course together, and got the same top grades. But, when we graduated, nobody seemed to care about our grades, so the best jobs we could find were as filing clerks.*
>
> *We worked really hard, and well, and after three years, we figured we were about to be promoted—but our jobs were replaced by a database system. We figured the future was in automation, so we got jobs in database administration.*

*There, we each managed to automate several of the company's key processes, so we figured we were going to get a pretty good reward. But, just about that time, the company decided to bring in an integrated off-the-shelf database system, and all our work was discarded.*

*We decided that the software industry was a better place to do meaningful work, so we got jobs as software developers in a fiery start-up company. We built a terrific system that we thought was going to replace the current product line. But just as we were ready to deliver it, the project was terminated. We learned that our project was only being used as a sales ploy to defer customers from buying the competitor's system until revisions to the old flagship system were finished.*

*From that experience, we figured that the significant jobs were in management, where we would know what was going on. We both got jobs as project managers working on enhancements to the flagship product. We did super jobs, and were sure we were slated for upper management and bonuses and stock options, but then the company was sold out from under us—to the same competitor we had been trying to beat. The flagship product was trashed, along with our enhancements.*

*And that's why we're back on the job market, looking for something significant to do.*

"That's really depressing," I said.

"You're right," Fanny confirmed, glumly.

"Why should it be depressing?" Felicity asked, gaily.

"Well, every time you thought you'd accomplished something, you found out it didn't really matter in the grand scheme of things."

"Precisely," Fanny moaned, frowning. "In the end, it doesn't matter to the universe what we do."

"Exactly," her sister chimed in. "Since it doesn't matter to the universe what we do, then it certainly doesn't matter if we pretend it *does* matter. So, I'm pretending that all of it did matter, and that makes me very happy!"

There I had it—two opposite laws deriving from identical experiences. On one hand, there was Fanny's Frowning Fatalism:

**In the end, nothing matters.**

On the other, there was Felicity's Feather Philosophy:

**Since nothing matters in the end, it doesn't matter if I pretend that it does matter.**

At the time, I didn't share Felicity's optimistic slant on life, so I wasn't quite ready to accept her philosophy. "But don't you know you're pretending that things matter? Doesn't that knowledge eventually depress you?"

"Oh, no," said Felicity. "Quite the contrary." And then she dealt me the fatal blow, one that's left me smiling forevermore:

**Since nothing matters in the end, it doesn't even matter if I pretend I'm not pretending.**

# 14

## *the hourglass*

Why is it we never have enough time to do it right,
but we always have enough time to do it over?
—Sign on a garage wall

Goaded by Virginia Satir's ". . . up until now" technique, I invented my personal Hourglass, representing my ability to make time for the good and to make good use of my time. The Hourglass is one of my most important tools because it's one that I tend to forget—even when I write about management, leadership, and consulting. Perhaps, as an old guy, I'd just like to believe that time isn't important so I don't have to think about how little I have left.

I was even going to leave my Hourglass out of this book, until Michelle, the same friend who tried to discourage me from writing this book in the first place, said, "Why are you avoiding the subject of *time*? Even in *The Secrets of Consulting*, the one glaring omission is a discussion of how you manage time."[1]

I tried to explain my way out of Michelle's grasp. "But I wrote a whole chapter on time management in *Becoming a Technical Leader*.[2] Why don't you read that?"

"I did read that. It was useful, but I want more. I want more *time!*"

"But I've already told you all I know," I argued, my protest growing weaker.

"Baloney! I've watched you, and you seem to have time that none of the rest of us has. I mean, where have you found the time to write all those books? How do you get all your projects done on time, and how do you help your clients do the same?"

"I don't know!" I squeaked.

"Well, you always tell us that the way you learn things is to write about them, to surface what you do know and organize it so others can understand. So, here's your big chance."

I was caught, snared in my own net, so I agreed to give it a try. First thing, I thought, I'd better use my Magnifying Glass and gather some data. As it happened, I was heavily involved in creating a new conference, and I decided to write about this project in order to surface some of my Hourglass strategies.

---

[1] Gerald M. Weinberg, *The Secrets of Consulting* (New York: Dorset House Publishing, 1985).

[2] See Gerald M. Weinberg, *Becoming a Technical Leader* (New York: Dorset House Publishing, 1986), pp. 249–57.

## COMPONENTS OF AN EFFECTIVE HOURGLASS

Weary of the same-old-same-old conferences, a group of consultants and I produced an annual event called AYE, or Amplifying Your Effectiveness, for our colleagues and clients. One of our main goals was to apply our own methods of amplifying effectiveness to the project itself, thereby learning what works and what doesn't. Of course, we were well aware of Pandora's Pox:

> **Nothing new ever works, but there's always hope that this time will be different.**[3]

Because many things would go wrong, despite our efforts and the eventual success of the conference itself, AYE offered me numerous opportunities to practice using my tools, especially my Hourglass.

I decided to keep a list of what sorts of events created delays and what Hourglass elements helped us manage time. Here's a small sample:

1. One project member's e-mail was delayed in cyberspace for several days. Messages arrived in the wrong order, producing confusion that produced more confusing messages. But the confusion only happened because we were too quick to respond to these e-mails. After the e-mail service was fixed, we discussed what happened and learned to take the time to notice e-mail dates before jumping to conclusions and replying. *Confusion wastes time.*

2. I was in such a hurry to provide an ability to pay conference bills that I forgot to sign one of two signature lines on a bank form establishing the project bank account, delaying bill payment. This could have caused rippling delays, but didn't, because people had their own budgets, could pay the bills, and had faith that they would be reimbursed. Here, The Hourglass took two common forms: trust of one another and a little extra money in the bank. *Haste wastes time. Trust is a substitute for time. So is money, if used properly.*

3. One host broke his hand, which was tough because he couldn't use his Braille reader. This delayed his essay

---

[3] *The Secrets of Consulting,* p. 142.

for our pre-conference book, *Amplifying Your Effectiveness*.[4] As it turned out, he wasn't the only one whose essay was delayed. The lesson here is to stop yourself from getting too excited about an unanticipated delay— at least until you find out whether or not it will actually delay the entire project. *Jumping to conclusions wastes time; so does blame.*

4.    Some security certificates (whatever they are) expired on my primary Web browser, and my attempt to update them crashed my system. This delayed some tasks on that browser for several days—but the effect was diminished because I had an alternative browser that I could use for most tasks. *Computers can waste time; backups can save it.*

5.    Several people took vacations. This wouldn't have been much of a problem if we'd thought to put these vacations in our plan. After the first few vacations, we corrected our error, and people informed each other in advance. *It's not the time off that wastes time; it's the lack of planning.*

6.    One host had a serious family situation and had to cut back on her participation until it was resolved. This meant a bigger, yet manageable, workload for several other people. Because we had allowed some slack, the schedule effect was minimal once our project manager reallocated the tasks. *Slack saves time; so does depending on dependable people.*

7.    Hosts who were not at our initial planning meeting had to be brought up to date—not just on our plans, but on the logic behind them. We hadn't planned for this, so it was a real delay. However, it made us rethink some of our logic before it was too late to change. *Indoctrinating new people takes time, but it's not wasted time.*

8.    One host who joined late had to be brought up to speed. Again, more delay, but he was a talented tester and subjected many of our plans to tests that we hadn't thought of. *Testing may seem costly in terms of time, but if done well, and early, it saves more than it costs.*

---

[4] Gerald M. Weinberg, James Bach, and Naomi Karten, eds., *Amplifying Your Effectiveness: Collected Essays* (New York: Dorset House Publishing, 2000).

9.   Hosts who joined late took up tasks that were dropped by the others. Educating them about the project turned out to be a sound investment. However, later in the project, we wouldn't have had time to make their education pay off. *Training is another one of those activities that seems to cost time, but actually saves time—if done early.*

10.   Our host phone and e-mail lists were out-of-date, at the start of the project, causing irritating delays until we fixed them. This contact information should have been established at the very beginning and maintained throughout, as it is necessary for a distributed project. *Errors waste time.*

11.   One host's son got sick, which took her attention away from AYE business for several weeks. I began to wonder impatiently why all these people were being so inconsiderate of our conference's problems. I wondered, Didn't they have plans? Didn't their plans take precedence over sickness—for themselves and their loved ones? *Impatience wastes time; so does failure to accept reality.*

12.   I found a strange new mole on my neck, and had what the doctor called minor surgery. Then she found another suspicious mole, and I had more minor surgery. Then I had a dental emergency. I began to understand about people's plans. Any plan that doesn't allow for human frailty is a defective plan. *It's not that the project doesn't fit the plan, it's that the plan doesn't fit the project.*

13.   We needed an essay from each host for the conference book, *Amplifying Your Effectiveness.* However, as I mentioned above, a few people were late with their material. Their failures to meet the schedule wouldn't have been so troublesome, but we had vowed that everybody would have an essay in the book. Consequently, getting the last essay was like trying to get that last number on your bingo card—and equally frustrating. We had created what I call a Bingo Bog—where you wallow while waiting for every last place to be filled. *Poor structures waste time; so do unreasonable expectations.*

14. Unfortunately, some of the essay drafts weren't up to our quality standards. They had to be recycled. We could have saved time by lowering our quality standards, but quality was one of the key goals of our conference. What good would it do to preach quality when we ourselves didn't practice it? *Time saved by failing to live up to your principles is not time saved at all; in fact, it leads to a wasted life.*

15. Our perfectionism resulted in occasional panic attacks. Learning to think about what was acceptable quality, rather than perfect quality, was a major cure. *Reasonableness saves enormous amounts of time.*

16. The Internet service provider that hosted our e-mail lists failed intermittently. We were able to bypass the convenience of group lists by maintaining our own project teams' lists. We realized that we had chosen our provider because it was the cheapest—a lesson for next time. *Money may not be able to buy happiness, but it can buy reliability, which can buy time.*

## Jerry's Iron Rule of Project Life

We had many more causes for delay, but I think I'll stop here—to save time. For now, I'd like to summarize the lessons, all of which are components of my Hourglass.

- God may have priorities that are higher than my project. I leave slack in my plan for acts of God.

- Perfectionism kills schedules; reasonableness saves them.

- Certain project structures make success as likely as winning the lottery. I search for and eliminate this Bingo Bog from my plans. Not only does this eliminate "bad luck," but it also lowers psychological pressure on me, which leads to "good luck."

- Quality is negotiable, but not infinitely negotiable.

- Plans are predictions; plan to test them early and often, and then adjust them.

- Machines fail. Software fails. People are even less reliable, but since they're more adaptable, they're handy to have around to back up the machine systems.

- If I have a single point of failure, it will fail at a single point in time. After that, if I have any brains at all, I'll remove it.

- Cross-training is one of the surest ways to protect against those single points of failure. Another reliable protection is a good asset-control system for all your project's assets. If you fail to maintain this system because "it doesn't seem important," you're sure to lose your assets.

- I'll never be aware in advance of all possible single points of failure, but if I do risk analysis, I'll be aware of many of them. This awareness will leave me more time to deal with the ones that escaped my risk analysis.

- I may not fully sympathize with other people's delays until they happen to me, but I try to learn to grant people a generous interpretation. This may calm me down sufficiently so that I can become part of the solution, rather than add my blaming behavior to the time problem.

- Finally, I often hear my clients tell me that their project will make its schedule "if everything works out right." Well, I've been in the project business for more than forty years now, and I've seen several thousand projects. I've never seen one in which "everything works out right."

This lack of data has led me to formulate Jerry's Iron Rule of Project Life:

**It always takes longer.**

Defy this Iron Rule at your peril. Plan for delays, and plan to be adaptable and forgiving when unplanned delays occur. You'll be more successful, and you may even be happier. Our AYE project was on schedule for its debut; we didn't have any rush or panic near the end; the conference was wonderful; and we're all rather happy about it, applying what we've learned to subsequent AYE events.[5]

---

[5] For more information on the Amplifying Your Effectiveness (AYE) Conference, visit www.ayeconference.com.

*Quick and Neat*

Although many things went wrong in the preparation for the first AYE conference, we could have had even more but for what I'd learned about managing time from my friend Norie Yasukawa. While I was working with her on a book, Norie was doing biological research on mouse populations, experiments in which it took only one careless setup step to kill all the mice or let them escape. Watching Norie taught me that the surest way to waste time is to throw caution to the winds, a principle that I call The Time Bomb:

**Time wounds all heels.**[6]

The Hourglass often reminds me that I have enough time to do it right. It also reminds me that anything worth doing is worth doing right. Therefore, it reminds me that if I'm short of time, there's no point in wasting time doing a shoddy job. I call this Norie's Neat Nostrum:

**There's no such thing as quick and dirty; if you want a quick job, make it a neat job.**

In the past, I've taken on a job that the customer wants shortened, only to get the customer reaction that I didn't do a very good job. Here are some instances when, to my regret, I've been tempted to forget my Hourglass:

- Short versions of workshops: The customer says, "Anything you can teach in four days, you can teach in three. Give me the quick-and-dirty version."

- Quick consulting: A client says, "We want you to transform this entire organization with a one-hour speech." I reply, "But I don't know how to do that." The client pauses a moment and says, "Okay, we'll give you two hours."

- Minimizing complaints: "I'm having a problem with one of my employees [or associates, or vendors]. I want ever so badly for it just to be over with, so I just want to deny that it's that important."

---

[6] *The Secrets of Consulting*, p. 147.

Of course, the same temptations arise in managing my own time, my resources, and indeed, my whole life. Because I always want to do things well, I take my time. I'm an intuitive, so if I hurry, I always forget some detail. The Hourglass reminds me to allow slack in my plans, such as they are, not for the things I didn't expect but for the things I didn't think of. The Hourglass reminds me that it's me—not the world out there—that foils *my* plans.

## Conscious Experience

In my work, I find that the rarest and most essential ingredient in designing a successful process is *conscious experience.* By conscious experience, I mean being *involved* but not quite *so* involved that I stop being *aware.* I take some time after the experience to reflect on what happened. What went well? What went poorly? What alternatives were left unexplored? What was the information flow? Who wasn't involved, and why? How did the environment influence the process? What did *I* personally do that was effective or ineffective?

Experience may be the best teacher, but experience won't teach me a thing if I don't approach it *consciously.* When I take the time to be conscious—which means to be fully present to *all* aspects of the situation—I always fear at first that I'm losing time. In the end, though, I always recapture that time, with interest.

When the process has to be done on a schedule, consciousness becomes even more important. If I fall asleep on even one task out of hundreds, I can destroy any schedule. I need a tenacious Hourglass tool to stay in control of time. At any point, because time wounds all heels, consciousness may be the first thing I lose when I'm in a hurry.

In short, hurry leads to loss of conscious attention, which then leads to loss of time. So, hurry ultimately leads to lost time. . . . Oh, that's "haste makes waste"—a cliché, but one I forget at the most critical times.

## Starting Right

One of those critical times in which I'm most prone to haste is at the beginning of something new. If I'm in a hurry to get started, my Hourglass reminds me that "not enough time" actually means "not important enough." I may be hurrying because I don't think a good start is that important. Because I've always viewed myself as an adaptable, creative person, I used to think that a careful start wasn't that important. If I left something off my to-do list, I could always make it up as I went along, so I was free to get started quickly.

I was right about the to-do list, but I was totally wrong about starting carelessly. My eyes were opened when my friend Leo Hepis showed me the greatest time-saving tool of all, his *To-Not-Do List*. At the start of every month, Leo sits down and lists all the things he's not going to worry about doing that month. What could be more time-saving than that?

In other words, the big reason you save time if you take time at the beginning is that it gives your Wisdom Box time to work and apply Cary's Crap Caution, which we saw in Chapter 2:

**Anything not worth doing is not worth doing right.**

Cary's Crap Caution has saved me countless hours that would have been wasted reading things that weren't worth reading, writing things that nobody wanted to read, doing administrative tasks that accomplished nothing, and cleaning up things that were destined to be thrown away.

But not everyone can accept Leo's To-Not-Do List as a useful time-saving tool. The most common objection I hear is that some problems get worse the longer we wait to address them effectively. This is a valid objection, so identify these problems and keep them off your To-Not-Do List. In fact, do them first.

The second most common objection I hear is usually put in the form of an anxious question: "What if you keep putting something on your list and it *never* gets done?" To answer this objection, I point out that there are two types of problems on the list—those that grow more important with time and those that grow less important. The ones that grow more important will eventually become important enough to be taken off the list.

The others? Well, if they keep getting less important, they will eventually become so unimportant that you can drop them altogether. The To-Not-Do List allows me to postpone doing those things that aren't so important today and *might* go away tomorrow. I call this principle Leo's Lazy Law:

**Never do today what might not have to be done tomorrow; in fact, never even think about doing it.**

What a time-saver!

## Stopping Right

Not all time is wasted at the start of things. Some of it is wasted by inefficiencies during the process, but that's not usually as important as the time that's wasted at the end—or, rather, after what *should* be the end but isn't. My Hourglass also represents my ability to remember to ask if it's time to stop. For example,

- Is it time to stop working on this assignment?

- Is the result good enough for its purpose?

- Is it time to stop working with a particular client?

- Is it time to stop being an independent consultant

    . . . because I have all the money I need?

    . . . because I'm just not making enough money?

    . . . because I'm not really getting what I wanted?

- Is it time to retire?

- Is it time to stop thinking all the time whether it's time to stop yet?

- Is it time to stop writing this chapter?

# 15

## *the oxygen mask*

Lord, grant that I may always
desire more than I can accomplish.
—Michelangelo Buonarroti

The Oxygen Mask is my symbol for a balanced and vital life, not just a balanced and vital moment.[1] It reminds me of my ability to breathe and my need to take care of myself before attempting to help others. My colleague Eileen Strider added the mask to my kit, reminding me of the safety instructions given on planes: "Before helping others with their mask, be sure your own mask is securely in place and operating properly."

I like to think I have something in common with great artists like Michelangelo, but what I seem to have most in common is the desire to accomplish more than I could ever accomplish—not painting great works of art, but restoring the great works of art who are my clients. My Oxygen Mask acts as a governor of this tendency, reminding me to operate from a healthy place—the place from which I'm most likely to be able to help others, rather than inflict help that may prove harmful should I crash and burn and fail to follow through.

The Oxygen Mask reminds me to use all of my other tools and to keep myself healthy and sane.

## WHY WE BURN OUT

This has been a dry, dry year in the forests of northern New Mexico, where I spend most of the year. Many, many tens of thousands of acres have been burned out by forest fires. Viewing some of these burned-out areas, I'm reminded of the thousands of burned-out consultants I've met in my career. I wanted to write a chapter about taking care of yourself, about preventing burnout, but I was too burned-out from evacuating our log cabin in the Santa Fe National Forest and then moving back when the immediate fire danger had passed (within one mile of us).

My wife, Dani, trains dog consultants—people who work with problem dogs and their problem owners—and she tells me that they burn out, too. Dani writes a regular column in *Forward*, the award-winning magazine of the National Association of Dog Obedience Instructors (NADOI). She, in fact, wrote a column on burnout, and I had a great idea. I would steal her column (not really stealing it, though, since this is a community property state), and see if I could adapt it for consultants

---

[1] Special appreciation goes to Dani Weinberg for coauthoring Chapter 15, and for everything else.

in general. She and I had already agreed that it would be fun to switch audiences once in a while—though I still haven't figured out what a management consultant could say to interest obedience instructors—except perhaps some tips on cleaning up messes.

If you're a new consultant, or if you're converting your speciality from one discipline to another, you probably don't know much about burnout. Switching roles (like switching audiences) can help prevent burnout, so you might even doubt that it's possible for someone to stop loving what they love so much. Be assured, though: Burnout happens!

Burnout is most likely to happen in mid-career: You've been a successful consultant for a few years, and you've mastered some conventional methods and developed variations that work well for your clients. You've worked out the logistics of contracting—how much work to take; what marketing, legal, and administrative help you need—and the basics of being on the road and adapting quickly to new work environments. In sum, you're very good at what you do, and you have quite a few years of experience under your belt.

Suddenly, you find yourself devastated by burnout!

How do you recognize burnout? How about apathy, sluggishness, lack of interest, low energy, frustration, helplessness, boredom, fatigue, hopelessness? Technical problems seem much more difficult to solve, and the solutions suddenly feel unrewarding. Clients seem stupid and stubborn.

A dog instructor colleague of Dani's, seized by burnout, put it succinctly: "I'm sick and tired of teaching people how to get their dogs to stop pooping on the living room rug." A contractor I know reminded me of this statement when he said, "How many more times am I going to have to recover key files that were never backed up?" These statements capture the sense of trivialization of what once seemed so important and valuable.

There are some obvious reasons why people burn out—for example, working too hard, trying to do too much, going too far beyond their physical and emotional limitations. Yet these are only the effects of some underlying issues that are the real source of burnout. Understanding these issues can help us understand why we overwork ourselves and drive ourselves into this unhappy state.

First, in the sections that follow, we'll look at "the Shoulds"—all the requirements and constraints that we feel are imposed on us and that eat away at our self-esteem. Then, we'll consider what happens when we are trapped in our own success and afraid to change. Finally, we'll examine some ways to turn these things around to our advantage—by actually cultivating the chaos that they produce in our lives.

## The Dreaded "Shoulds"

When I feel that I'm being forced to do something I don't want to do, or when I feel that my options have been reduced to zero, or when I cannot see a way out of what appears to be a very tight box—that's when I'm heading for burnout.

Think about times when you've felt your autonomy was seriously threatened, when someone else was calling the shots—and those shots were nowhere near your own. For example, I have a colleague who is assigned to work on the graveyard shift every night of the week because, as his client says, "you're our best emergency man." Another colleague allowed the sponsors of his C++ workshop to enroll forty students—even though the course was designed for twelve—saying it was "because of our high dropout rate." (I wonder why!) Another colleague is responsible for reporting software test results to a group of programmers with bad attitudes because, as his client says, "there's no one else who will work with them."

Now, it is possible that these consultants prefer working through the night, or teaching large classes, or interacting with nasty people. But if these are not their preferences, they've bought into some activities that will very likely lead to burnout. They've failed to use their Yes/No Medallions, and they're going to pay the price.

I learned a lot about burnout when I was in college. I had a full-time job washing dishes because that way I got free meals (if you could call them that) as a perk. I was taking an overfull load of premed courses because my mother wanted me to become a doctor. I was pledging to a fraternity whose members believed the more abusive grunt work they assigned, the better frat brothers the pledges would become. I complied because a good friend said the fraternity house was the only place to live on campus. Eventually, I wound up dropping out of school and dropping into the hospital. That's burnout.

My problem was rooted in what I call "the Shoulds." I felt that I *should* be a premed because my parents wanted it and since doctors had helped me, I *should* repay the world. I believed that I *should* settle for a career in medicine, rather than in computing, because I *shouldn't* be selfish. I thought I *should* belong to the fraternity because my friend there had encouraged me to continue school. I thought I *should* work my way through school because I *shouldn't* take money from other people. And, once I started, I thought that I *should* finish what I had started, as painful as it was. I was trapped in the Shoulds—in other words, my survival rules were killing me!

I've stood at the brink of burnout many times since those days. For example, as a writer, I would get an unfavorable review of a manuscript, and I would catch myself in the Believe-the-Expert trap. You know that one: "He's the expert, so I should do what he says."

As a teacher, I've risked burnout by agreeing to do what my best judgment told me was not right for me—for example, allowing too many students to take a class ("I *should* accept everyone"), tolerating students who never did the homework ("I *shouldn't* force anyone"), using at my client's request techniques I didn't care for ("I *should* be flexible"), and on and on.

Unfortunately, one of the symptoms of burnout is the inability to reach out for help. That means that when I most need emotional support and new ideas, I am least likely to look for them ("I *should* be able to do it myself"). Burnout is fundamentally a state of very low self-esteem. When I'm there, I see myself as not deserving. Asking for help and support seems, in that state of being, to broadcast my own worthlessness and incompetence.

## Competence Can Lead to Burnout

Over the years, I have struggled to become more competent, so as to avoid getting trapped by the Shoulds. But competence itself isn't a sure cure for low self-esteem, and curiously, it can even precipitate burnout.

When I'm good at what I do, I usually get lots of reinforcement. I get wonderful client evaluations, my job offers increase as my satisfied clients spread the word, and I attract much more interesting and better-paying clients. When something goes wrong, with anything, I'm the first one my clients call on to solve it.

The first consequence of this kind of success is the Pile-On Dynamic.[2] The more successes I have, the more work I get; and the more work I get, the more successes I have. My clients are more likely to offer assignments to me first, choice assignments that I have a hard time resisting. Pretty soon, I'm loaded beyond my ability to sustain, but because my clients' requests are so flattering, I struggle to sustain my efforts long past the time I should have started saying, "Thank you, but not this time." Then, I burn out.

The Pile-On Dynamic works its evil consequences because I respond to reinforcement. Dog-training instructors understand this; whatever training methodology they use, reinforcement is an important element to increase the behavior they want in students and their dogs.

---

[2] To learn more about the Pile-On Dynamic, see Gerald M. Weinberg, *Quality Software Management, Vol. 1: Systems Thinking* (New York: Dorset House Publishing, 1992), pp. 256–58.

Reinforcement is an essential part of the learning process. The same thing works for human beings, particularly for those of us who work on contract. I don't wag my tail for dried liver treats, but I sure respond to money, interesting assignments, and praise.

If the rate at which I get such reinforcement is too low, I don't experience enough feeling of success. As a consequence, I tend to shut down and maybe even give up—this is burnout from lack of reinforcement. Having learned the hard way about this brand of burnout, I now know I have to seek reinforcement. I make sure I get paid enough, and work on interesting assignments. When I'm done with an assignment, I ask my clients if they're satisfied with my work. So, being as experienced as I am, I ought to be getting enough reinforcement to prevent burnout entirely, right?

No, not right, because it's possible to get *too much* reinforcement. For one thing, if my competence is overly rewarded, I'll doubt and discount the value of the reinforcement. Or, when I become really good at what I do and begin to reap the fruits of success, I may hesitate about changing anything, say, in my workshop handouts—except maybe the color of the cover. I become overly sensitive to any chance comment that might be critical, and I worry about the slightest confusion a client displays when I make a suggestion. I begin to pick and choose clients and situations more carefully until all my clients are true believers. I become more and more risk-aversive. After all, it's working, so why change anything?

Soon, I notice that I'm not looking forward to assignments anymore. I start criticizing and making fun of my clients with my colleagues. I lose patience more easily and find myself more often in a grouchy mood. I no longer invite colleagues to observe my work and give me feedback. Why bother? Things are going well, and there's no need to change anything.

And yet . . . something is not right. I don't feel good about myself or about my work. I might even start to have health problems, be more accident-prone, start canceling appointments more easily for "health" or "weather" reasons.

Burnout is all too common in the consulting business, but we need not be as helpless as small animals trapped by a forest fire. Help comes from understanding how burnout happens, and from some paradoxical actions—much like the intentional setting of forest fires to limit the spread of bigger fires.

CULTIVATING CHAOS

Virginia Satir's Change Model describes how change and learning happen.[3] To understand burnout, we need to look at the stage called Old Status Quo. This is the place where my competence and success have been well established, and all I'm doing now is repeating myself endlessly. As dulling and depressing as it is to be in Old Status Quo, I still prefer the misery of the familiar to the uncertainty of stepping out into a new place. When I'm in Old Status Quo, I'll choose pain over risk any day. The pain might be only at the level of being bored, or it might be manifested as actual physical pain or even illness. But I hang on anyway because my routine is tried and true and safe—in that sense, at least. My Oxygen Mask is supposed to remind me that this kind of "safe" is like the safety of being dead—I'm in no danger of changing, if you don't count decaying.

Many people remain in Old Status Quo all their lives. They finish school, get married, find a job, and stay there forever, just counting the days until retirement. For consultants, though, this is not the usual course. They may have started along this path, but perhaps they were rudely shoved out of Old Status Quo by what Virginia Satir called a *foreign element*.

A foreign element is anything that comes along that forces you to try something different because the risk now feels like losing everything you have. For example, you may have a wonderful job as a supervisor in a fine company, only to hear one day that the company has been acquired by a company that's less than fine. You're told that everything will remain the same, and it seems to, for quite a while, but one day, the new company announces a downsizing, and you're handed a pink slip. Now, that's a rude awakening! Suddenly, you become aware that you've been hanging on for a long time—and now you're forced to let go. That awful awareness marks the beginning of burnout.

Much as you would like to remain in the Old Status Quo, that decision has been taken out of your hands. You might try to hang on by negotiating with your new boss, or by begging for more time—just another ten years!—but finally you have to face up to the foreign element and do something else.

And now, instead of the mind-dulling comfort of Old Status Quo, you're thrown into the next stage: Chaos, also known as Burnout Supreme. Nothing makes sense anymore. There are either too many or too few options out there. Every time you think you have a solution, a

---

[3] To learn more about the Satir Change Model, see Gerald M. Weinberg, *Quality Software Management, Vol. 4: Anticipating Change* (New York: Dorset House Publishing, 1997).

dozen more possibilities or doubts pop up in your mind. You feel as if you're sailing a small sailboat in the middle of a rough and stormy sea. At moments, the clouds part and the downpour stops, but then it starts again even more forcefully. You feel—well, "crazy" is a good word for the Chaos stage!

Chaos feels very different from Old Status Quo—in fact, almost the opposite. It's not dull but agitating. It's not safe but scary. It's not depressing but turbulent with energy. There is no order. You feel off-balance and confused.

But look at all the new ideas floating around in the churning waves! Notice the possibilities for creativity and for letting go of old assumptions and beliefs. The worst has happened: Your sailboat has been torn apart by the storm. But look at all the wonderful bits and pieces of wood, canvas, plastic, and metal that are suddenly available to you.

This is the essence and power of Chaos. In Chaos, we rediscover our ability to learn and grow. Chaos is where we find our willingness to risk and to play. For example, let's go back to the case of the lost job. Hit with that Foreign Element, you might decide to take a break from supervising and try something you've been thinking about for years. Perhaps you've wanted to go back to designing software, but when you still had a steady supervisory job, you couldn't afford the time or financial risks. Or maybe you'd like to try your hand at consulting.

I know many people who have found the freedom, in the Chaos of losing their day jobs, to do marvelous things. Jacob, for example, decided to take a few months off and write a book about his design methods. Wendel started teaching project management classes at the local community college. Patsy took a consulting assignment in Italy, a place she'd always dreamed of visiting. And Evie became a software tester, something she had always found intriguing but, as a highly respected software developer, had never dared to do. As for me, I first started consulting full-time when I was burned out from teaching at a university.

In these examples, we all used Chaos to our benefit, to put burnout behind us and to recreate our professional lives so that we could once again make important contributions. Risk-taking, inventiveness, and learning all come out of Chaos.

*Getting the Most Out of Chaos*

Because burnout comes from the perceived constriction of choice—the Shoulds—you can use Chaos to take back control of your life. The first step is to find support and to practice self-care—to put on your own Oxygen Mask so you'll have time to breathe and start using your other self-esteem tools.

- Value yourself, your beliefs, and your ideas. Use your Wishing Wand to discover your bottom line. Avoid placating and putting the wishes of others before your own.

- Trust yourself. Don't just know your bottom line; honor it. If something isn't right for you, flip your Medallion to NO.

- Know yourself and your personal style and preferences. Use your Mirror. When you take time to relax, be sure that you're really relaxing. For example, relaxing for me means physical activity, like a hike or some strength training, not resting (inactivity). For you, it might mean sitting down with a good science fiction novel (which I love, too).

- Practice self-care by honoring your own physical and emotional limitations. For example, maybe you can use your Telescope to find qualified colleagues to whom you can pass attractive assignments that are piling on you.

- Take a break. Getting away from the daily routine, even if it's just for a day or two, can be refreshing. Make good use of your free time to do something entirely different. And, if you don't have any free time, you'd better make some! That's what your Hourglass is for.

- Use your Courage Stick and actively seek the support you need from others. Talk to other consultants, exchange stories, articulate complaints, verbalize your feelings and concerns about problem clients or assignments. Be open to ideas and suggestions that your colleagues offer. Talk and listen!

- Because reinforcement issues are also a breeding ground for burnout, respect your need for meaningful, appropriate, and nourishing reinforcement. When you use your Mirror to get feedback, you rebuild your self-esteem.

- Remind yourself of your successes by using your Fish-Eye Lens to see the whole picture, not just this burned-out moment. Provide your own perspective and reinforcement by putting those "feel good" letters from satisfied clients in a scrapbook—something that can also be useful when you need references. But remember to look at them when you're feeling low, not just when you're trying to convince a prospect of your value!

- Recognize your boredom as Old Status Quo—and then move on. Use your Courage Stick to give up the comfort of familiarity for the riskiness of growth. You have a Golden Key, and you know how to use it.

- Ask for emotional support when you need it. A sounding board or a soft shoulder might be all you need. Seek this support from people who do more than just tell you how great you are. This is your informed Heart listening to their informed Hearts.

- Cultivate and cherish the Chaos in which you find yourself. Experience it as a place to restore, refresh, and rebuild motivation and excitement.

- Put on your Detective Hat and use your Magnifying Glass to seek out new ideas—the wilder the better. Brainstorm with friends and colleagues. And then—just try it!

- Let your Egg remind you to learn something new, add it to all the other things you know, and try it with a client. Give yourself some Carabiner protection by telling your client that this is a new idea. Most clients really appreciate the opportunity to participate in guided experiments and will respect you for your willingness to learn. If this one doesn't, consider it a sign that there may be a burnout in your future if you stay there too long.

These days, when I start to feel the symptoms of burnout, I remind myself that there's no way but up, if I use the tools available to me. Even though it may feel as if the walls are closing in on me, I try to focus on the many possibilities and new doors that Chaos opens. To find and open those doors takes awareness, understanding, courage, and support. And having been through this cycle, I become an even better consultant because of the help I can give my clients when I see them struggle.

And, increasingly, I use my entire tool kit to lessen the chance of burnout in the first place. I know I have all the tools I need, and looking out my cabin window, I know one more important thing. From watching the forests around me recover from devastating fires, I know that nature has a special healing power. I don't need to burn myself out trying to escape burnout. I've got nature on my side.

# Epilogue

**When I examine myself and my methods of thought,
I come to the conclusion that the gift of fantasy
has meant more to me than any talent
for abstract, positive thinking.
—Albert Einstein**

Originally, I thought of my self-esteem tool kit—with Virginia Satir's tools and those that I've added—as a purely mental construct. With age and experience, however, I've come to realize the power of physical tokens that represent the tools—like the items the Wizard gave Dorothy and her friends. Over the years, I've amassed a wonderful collection of various representations of my tools, so I can play Wizard, too.

## THE TRAVELING TOOL KIT

Among my most valued representations is a wearable tool kit that a member of one of my Systems Effectiveness Management groups, a physician we call Dr. Kate, made for each other member of her group. Another member, Elisabeth, wrote about what happened when she passed it on:

> *I wanted to share a story with all of you about the power of self-esteem kits, and to thank you—Dani, Jerry, Jean, and Dr. Kate—for making possible the original portable self-esteem kit that I gave away. With each self-esteem kit that is given, it seems lives are changed.*
>
> *Dr. Kate gave me a tiny portable self-esteem kit: seven appropriately shaped charms in a tiny clear box.*
>
> *My friend and employee Melissa was having a difficult time with a coworker. At a loss for how to help her, I remembered Kate's tiny self-esteem kit.*

*I presented it to Melissa, explaining each tool, one by one. Melissa was moved. A few weeks later, when I asked her if she was using the kit, she beamed as she told me how she'd used it.*

*It's a year later, now. I just had lunch with Melissa the other day, and she shared an amazing story with me. She refers to the self-esteem kits as "boxes" (for the handy-dandy portable-sized clear case Kate used) and has been passing them on. Her story is in her own words, below:*

> *A friend of mine was having a very rough time. I wasn't sure how to help, but I made a box just like the one you gave me, adding a fairy so that she'd always know that the box was made just for her by someone who cared very much.*
>
> *A few weeks later, she entered drug rehabilitation.*
>
> *After much hard work, she was ready to graduate from her group. As her graduation gift, she made a box for each participant and added a small scale to remind everyone of the balance they needed to stay away from drugs.*
>
> *People from all walks of life were in her group, including ex-convicts—gruff, burly men who lived hard, cold lives. Afraid they'd laugh at her gift, my friend readied herself for what might come and gave each member a box. Instead of jeering or disregarding their small boxes, the convicts held the tiny charms carefully, some smiling and thanking her, while others just cried.*

I cry, too, when I receive gifts. I cried when I received these stories. At the time, I was searching for the perfect ending to this book, and this gift arrived just in time.

Perhaps you know people who are searching. Perhaps what they're searching for is a self-esteem tool kit. For a gift like this, you don't even have to wait for their birthday.

# Listing of Laws, Rules, and Principles

*The Antiseptic Absurdity:* If it hurts, it must be good for you. Good food takes time. If they tell you it *must* be good for you because it hurts, get yourself a different consultant. (p. 17)

*The As-If Technique:* If you *did* have feelings, what would they be like? What kinds of feelings do you think other people have? (pp. 90, 91)

*The Background Blindfold:* The fish is always the last to see the water. (p. 125)

*The Body-Brain Behest:* Trust your body, then your brain. (p. 140)

*Boulding's Backward Basis:* Things are the way they are because they got that way. (p. 127)

*Brown's Brilliant Bequest:* Words are often useful, but it always pays to listen to the music (especially your own internal music). (p. 128)

*Carl's Constructive Corollary:* Use feedback as a reminder, not a reproach. (p. 101)

*Cary's Crap Caution:* Anything not worth doing is not worth doing right, or, Never gift wrap garbage. (p. 13)

*The Choice Charm:* People are there because they have *chosen* to be there. (p. 156)

*Clarke's Third Law:* Any sufficiently advanced technology is indistinguishable from magic. (p. 154)

*The Coward's Credo:* Courage is not a feeling, but an outer appearance. (p. 35)

*Crisis Bias:* When in danger or in doubt, run in circles, scream, and shout. (p. 64)

*The Crooked Channel Cleanser:* When you're having trouble understanding what you're receiving, first check that your channel is congruent. (p. 132)

*Dani's Decider:* When you stop learning new things, it's time to move on. (p. 26)

*The Data Question:* What specifically did I see or hear that gave me that impression of this person? (p. 114)

*The Detective's Fifth Rule:* Confusion favors the established order, so use your confusion to find the culprit. (p. 72)

*The Detective's First Rule:* When you're looking for problems, don't be mesmerized by the first one you find. (p. 66)

*The Detective's Fourth Rule:* If you can't understand where the questions are coming from, they're probably coming from an agenda someone doesn't want you to know about. (p. 69)

*The Detective's Second Rule:* If you're shot dead and stabbed dead, you're no more dead than if you're just shot dead. (p. 67)

*The Detective's Third Rule:* Get the information you need from the questions they ask you. (p. 68)

*The Dismal Theorem of Middlemen:* Negotiating the heck out of a deal with middlemen is unlikely to improve your situation, because *they're professionals and you're an amateur.* (p. 51)

*Don's Deviance Derivation:* If it's too regular, it's not an observation; it's a formulation. (p. 122)

*Fanny's Frowning Fatalism:* In the end, nothing matters. (p. 159)

*The Fast-Food Fallacy:* No difference plus no difference plus no difference plus . . . eventually equals a clear difference. (p. 19)

*Felicity's Feather Philosophy:* Since nothing matters in the end, it doesn't matter if I pretend that it does matter. Since nothing matters in the end, it doesn't even matter if I pretend I'm not pretending. (p. 160)

*The First Law of Bad Management,* or *The First Law of Bad Consulting:*
When something isn't working, do more of it. (p. 121)

*The First Law of Good Consulting:* When something isn't working,
do something else. (p. 121)

*The Five-Minute Rule:* Clients always know how to solve their
problems, and always tell the solution in the first five minutes. (p. 127)

*The Foreground Fantasy:* The fish is always the first to notice the air.
(p. 126)

*The Fraidycat Formula:* If your fear of doing A is greater than your
fear of doing B, then you do B. (p. 37)

*Freeble's Feeling Filter: Anything* I shouldn't be doing, I shouldn't be
doing. Period. (p. 14)

*Getting the Most Out of Chaos* (pp. 180–81):

- Value yourself, your beliefs, and your ideas.

- Trust yourself.

- Know yourself and your personal style and preferences.

- Practice self-care.

- Take a break.

- Actively seek the support you need from others.

- Respect your need for meaningful, appropriate, and
  nourishing reinforcement.

- Remind yourself of your successes.

- Recognize your boredom as Old Status Quo—and then
  move on.

- Ask for emotional support when you need it.

- Cultivate and cherish the Chaos in which you find yourself.

- Seek out new ideas—the wilder the better.

- Learn something new, add it to all the other things you
  know, and try it with a client.

*The Golden Lock:* I'd like to learn something new, but what I already know pays too well. (p. 25)

*The Goody Goody Guide:* If you *must* have *everyone* like you, get out of the consulting business. (p. 81)

*Gordon's Law of First Consulting:* Don't say yes to a client's first offer, but never say no. (p. 78)

*The Happy Theorem:* Regardless of the agency's cut, if you're unhappy, they're impoverished. (p. 52)

*The Heart Test:* If you don't care about them or their problems, don't consult for them. (p. 94)

*The Helpful Model:* No matter how it looks, everyone is trying to be helpful. (p. 101)

*The Housewife Assumption:* Don't assume that your clients have nothing better to do than wait by the phone for your call. (p. 61)

*The Human Hypotenuse Hypothesis:* When one person, C, separates your heart, A, from another's, B, choose the shortest path between A and B. (p. 88)

*The Hypotenuse Hypothesis:* When a triangle separates you from your data, choose the hypotenuse. (pp. 63, 88)

*The Incongruence Insight:* When words and music don't go together, they point to a missing element. (p. 130)

*The Informed Heart Test:* If someone requires you to die trying to help them, you don't want to help them. (p. 94)

*The Inverse Gilded Rule:* If something's faked, it must need fixing. (p. 131)

*Isabelle's Initial Indication:* You never start with a blank slate. (p. 117)

*Jerry's Iron Rule of Project Life:* It always takes longer. (p. 167)

*Kenny's Law of Auto Repair:* The part requiring the most consistent repair or replacement will be housed in the most inaccessible location. (p. 102)

*Knaomi's Knowledge Knockout:* Experience is not just the best teacher, it's the only teacher. Experience may be the only teacher, but it doesn't necessarily teach anything. (p. 149)

*The Law of Grape Jelly:* Nobody ever bothers to complain about grape jelly. If you don't expect too much, you'll never be disappointed. (p. 4)

*The Law of the Hammer:* The child who receives a hammer for Christmas will discover that everything needs pounding. (p. 63)

*The Law of Raspberry Jam:* The wider you spread it, the thinner it gets. (p. 2)

*The Law of Strawberry Jam:* As long as it has lumps, you can never spread it too thin. (p. 3)

*The Law of Unavoidably Messy Peculiarity:* One person's help is another's hardship. One person's lump is another person's lumps. (p. 118)

*LeGuin's Law:* When action grows unprofitable, gather information. When information grows unprofitable, sleep. (p. 64)

*Leo's Lazy Law:* Never do today what might not have to be done tomorrow; in fact, never even think about doing it. (p. 170)

*The Life Law:* Better to live succeeding than to die trying. (p. 94)

*Loftus' Law:* Some people manage by the book, even though they don't know who wrote the book or even which book it is. (p. 40)

*The Lump Law:* If we want to learn anything, we musn't try to learn everything. (p. 4)

*The Magic Double Bind:* If it's indistinguishable from magic, how do I know it won't go away next time? (p. 154)

*The Main Maxim:* What you don't know may not hurt you, but what you don't remember always does. (p. 19)

*Mana Model:* Certain people have big magic (mana) and certain people don't. (p. 147)

*Marvin's Fourth Great Secret:* Whatever the client is doing, advise something else. (p. 41)

*Matthew's Yea/Nay Signal:*  Honest, reliable people don't need to qualify their yeas and nays with declarations of their honesty and reliability, and everyone instinctively knows this. (p. 79)

*The Mercenary Maxim:*  One of the best ways to lose lots of money is to do something only for the money. (p. 18)

*Monica's Marvelous Mirror:*  Negotiating a contract is a marvelous opportunity for both parties to take a good look at themselves. (p. 98)

*Monica's Mirror Monition:*  Some people do not wish to look in a marvelous mirror. (p. 98)

*The Nedlog Rule:*  As they do unto others, they will eventually do unto you. (p. 67)

*Norie's Neat Nostrum:*  There's no such thing as quick and dirty; if you want a quick job, make it a neat job. (p. 168)

*Pandora's Pox:*  Nothing new ever works, but there's always hope that this time will be different. (p. 163)

*The Parallel Paradox:*  If you're too much like your clients, you don't attract them; if you're too different, you frighten them away. (p. 91)

*Parson's Peculiarity Principle:*  If they're acting peculiarly, maybe they're reacting to something peculiar; maybe it's me. (p. 141)

*The Perfect Poise Paradox:*  If you want to stay incongruent, try to be *perfectly* congruent. (p. 137)

*Polanski's Corollary:*  Don't bother looking where everyone is pointing. (p. 25)

*Polanski's Personal Pointer:*  Whenever you believe that a subject has nothing for you, it probably has something for you. (p. 25)

*Polanski's Pointer:*  If they're *absolutely sure* it's not there, it's probably there. (p. 24)

*The Qualified-but-Quiet Quandary:*  The more congruent you become, the more you have to watch what you say. (p. 147)

*The Railroad Counter-Paradox:* When service is too good, the suppliers may never hear about it, and thus they drop the service. (p. 60)

*The Railroad Paradox:* Because the service is bad, the request for better service is denied. (p. 60)

*Redding's Reading Rule:* Never read anything that isn't worth reading. (p. 12)

*The Response Pattern:* Center, enter, turn. (p. 112)

*The Rule of Restrained Rationality:* Don't be rational; be reasonable. Not everything that sounds wise is wise. (p. 16)

*Satir's Soft Spurn:* 1. Show genuine appreciation, in words, tone, and body language. 2. Give a regretful, but clear, no, without excuses. 3. Indicate an opening to some other relationship in the future. (p. 77)

*Satir's Three Universal Questions* (p. 104):

- How do I happen to be here? (Past)
- How do I feel about being here? (Present)
- What would I like to have happen? (Future)

*Satir's Win/Lose/Learn Principle:* If you're congruent, you might win, or you might lose, but you can always learn. (p. 147)

*Secret Number One:* There are no secrets. Everyone can observe human behavior. (p. 103)

*Sherby's Fourth Law:* If you're using anything more than fourth-grade arithmetic, you're probably doing it wrong! (p. 71)

*Sparks's Law of Problem Solution:* The chances of solving a problem decline the closer you get to finding out who was the cause of the problem. (p. 124)

*Starr's Surrogate Syndrome:* No matter how much you or they would like it, you can't be congruent for someone else. (p. 148)

*The Sucker Syndrome:* It's easiest to fool the people who know everything. (p. 18)

*Sweeny's Teeny Weeny Signature Statute:* If you want a meaningful commitment, don't whine, sign. (p. 100)

*The Ted Williams Principle:* If you don't think too good, don't think too much. (p. 71)

*The Telescope Focusing List* (pp. 113–14):

1. Centering

2. Environment

3. Recording

4. Resemblance

5. Projecting

6. Pigeonhole

7. Mind Reading

8. History

9. Hearsay

10. Sharing

*The Three-Finger Rule:* When you point a finger at someone, notice where the other three fingers are pointing. (p. 96)

*The Time Bomb:* Time wounds all heels. (p. 168)

*The Time Wasters* (pp. 163–66):

- Confusion wastes time.

- Haste wastes time. Trust is a substitute for time. So is money, if used properly.

- Jumping to conclusions wastes time; so does blame.

- Computers can waste time; backups can save it.

- It's not the time off that wastes time; it's the lack of planning.

- Slack saves time; so does depending on dependable others.

- Indoctrinating new people takes time, but it's not wasted time.

- Testing may seem costly in terms of time, but if done well, and early, it saves more than it costs.

- Training is another one of those activities that seems to cost time, but actually saves time—if done early.

- Errors waste time.

- Impatience wastes time; so does failure to accept reality.

- It's not that the project doesn't fit the plan, it's that the plan doesn't fit the project.

- Poor structures waste time; so do unreasonable expectations.

- Time saved by failing to live up to your principles is not time saved at all; in fact, it leads to a wasted life.

- Reasonableness saves enormous amounts of time.

- Money may not be able to buy happiness, but it can buy reliability, which can buy time.

*The Ultimately Dismal Theorem:* If you don't know what you want, you're not very likely to get it. (p. 55)

*The Utterly Dismal Theorem of Middlemen:* The harder you try to improve your contract by getting a good negotiator as your middleman, the worse it gets. (p. 51)

*Weiner's Law of Libraries:* There are no answers, only cross-references. (p. 64)

# Bibliography

Bullock, James, Gerald M. Weinberg, and Marie Benesh, eds. *Roundtable on Project Management: A SHAPE Forum Dialogue.* New York: Dorset House Publishing, 2001.

Burnet, M., and D.O. White. *Natural History of Infectious Disease.* London: Cambridge University Press, 1972.

Butler, Pamela E. *Talking to Yourself: Learning the Language of Self-Affirmation.* San Francisco: Harper San Francisco, 1991.

Clarke, Arthur C. *Profiles of the Future: An Inquiry into the Limits of the Possible.* New York: HarperCollins, 1973.

Crum, Tom F. *The Magic of Conflict.* New York: Touchstone, Simon & Schuster, 1987.

Darby III, Joseph B. "Law and Tax: It's Time to Take Non-Compete Agreements Seriously." *Contract Professional* (July-August 1998), p. 45.

Gause, Donald C., and Gerald M. Weinberg. *Are Your Lights On? How to Figure Out What the Problem Really Is.* New York: Dorset House Publishing, 1990.

———. *Exploring Requirements: Quality Before Design.* New York: Dorset House Publishing, 1989.

Goffman, Erving. *Asylums.* Garden City, N.Y.: Doubleday & Co., 1961.

Kaplan, Abraham. *The Conduct of Inquiry: Methodology for Behavioral Science.* San Francisco: Chandler Publishing, 1964.

LeGuin, Ursula K. *The Left Hand of Darkness.* New York: Harper & Row, 1980.

Russell, Bertrand. *The Collected Stories of Bertrand Russell.* London: Allen & Unwin, 1972.

Seashore, C., E. Seashore, and G.M. Weinberg. *What Did You Say? The Art of Giving and Receiving Feedback.* North Attleboro, Mass.: Douglas Charles Press, 1992. Contact Bingham House Books at 10001 Windstream Drive, Suite 902, Columbia, MD 21044.

Stevens, J. *The Secrets of Aikido.* Boston: Shambhala, 1995.

Suzuki, Shunryu. *Zen Mind, Beginner's Mind.* New York: Weatherhill, 1960.

Weinberg, Gerald M. *Becoming a Technical Leader.* New York: Dorset House Publishing, 1986.

————. "Experiments in Problem Solving." Ph.D. Thesis, University of Michigan, 1965.

————. *An Introduction to General Systems Thinking: Silver Anniversary Edition.* New York: Dorset House Publishing, 2001.

————. *The Psychology of Computer Programming: Silver Anniversary Edition.* New York: Dorset House Publishing, 1998.

————. *Quality Software Management, Vol. 1: Systems Thinking.* New York: Dorset House Publishing, 1992.

————. *Quality Software Management, Vol. 2: First-Order Measurement.* New York: Dorset House Publishing, 1993.

————. *Quality Software Management, Vol. 3: Congruent Action.* New York: Dorset House Publishing, 1994.

————. *Quality Software Management, Vol. 4: Anticipating Change.* New York: Dorset House Publishing, 1997.

————. *Rethinking Systems Analysis and Design.* New York: Dorset House Publishing, 1988.

————. *The Secrets of Consulting.* New York: Dorset House Publishing, 1985.

————, James Bach, and Naomi Karten, eds. *Amplifying Your Effectiveness: Collected Essays*. New York: Dorset House Publishing, 2000.

Weinberg, Gerald M., Marie Benesh, and James Bullock, eds. *Roundtable on Technical Leadership: A SHAPE Forum Dialogue*. New York: Dorset House Publishing, 2002.

# Index

**Build Your Weinberg Library with Dorset House**

*Learn more at www.dorsethouse.com/authors/gerald_weinberg.html.*

✔ **Amplifying Your Effectiveness**, edited by Gerald M. Weinberg, James Bach, and Naomi Karten: Seventeen successful software consultants pool their best techniques for amplifying the effectiveness of software engineers and managers. New and previously published essays are represented, covering topics in personal empowerment, interpersonal interaction, mastering projects, and changing the organization.
   *ISBN: 0-932633-47-1 ©2000 160 pages softcover*

✔ **Are Your Lights On?** by Donald C. Gause and Gerald M. Weinberg: A breakthrough in creative problem solving, this book will help you improve your thinking power. First published in 1982, it is now considered a cult classic.
   *ISBN: 0-932633-16-1 ©1990 176 pages softcover*

✔ **Becoming a Technical Leader**, by Gerald M. Weinberg: Shows you how to evaluate and improve your skills in terms of innovation, motivation, and organization. Learn how to gain organizational power and plan personal change.
   *ISBN: 0-932633-02-1 ©1986 304 pages softcover*

✔ **Exploring Requirements**, by Donald C. Gause and Gerald M. Weinberg: The quintessential guide to the most important part of the product development process.
   *ISBN: 0-932633-13-7 ©1989 320 pages hardcover*

✔ **Handbook of Walkthroughs, Inspections, and Technical Reviews**, by Daniel P. Freedman and Gerald M. Weinberg: This lively, question-and-answer handbook helps you spot and eliminate defects—*before* customers find them.
   *ISBN: 0-932633-19-6 ©1990 464 pages hardcover*

✔ **An Introduction to General Systems Thinking: Silver Anniversary Edition**, by Gerald M. Weinberg: Use this book to dispel the mental fog that clouds problem-solving. Originally published in 1975, this classic text on systems theory has been used in courses and seminars world-wide.
   *ISBN: 0-932633-49-8 ©2001 304 pages hardcover*

✔ **The Psychology of Computer Programming, Silver Anniversary Edition**, by Gerald M. Weinberg: This landmark 1971 classic is reprinted with chapter-by-chapter commentary and a new Preface from the author. Long regarded as one of the first books to pioneer a people-oriented approach to computing, it remains strikingly pertinent to today's state of the profession.
   *ISBN: 0-932633-42-0 ©1998 360 pages softcover*

✔ **Quality Software Management, Vol. 1: Systems Thinking**, by Gerald M. Weinberg, presents potent, practical advice for tackling the first requirement for developing quality software: learning to think correctly—about problems, solutions, and quality itself.
   *ISBN: 0-932633-22-6 ©1992 336 pages hardcover*

✔ **Quality Software Management, Vol. 2: First-Order Measurement**, by Gerald M. Weinberg, teaches the fundamental techniques for observing project progress and using measurement to improve software quality.
   *ISBN: 0-932633-24-2 ©1993 360 pages hardcover*

✔ **Quality Software Management, Vol. 3: Congruent Action**, by Gerald M. Weinberg, shows how managers can put the concepts of good software engineering into action by managing themselves first.
   *ISBN: 0-932633-28-5 ©1994 328 pages hardcover*

✔ **Quality Software Management, Vol. 4: Anticipating Change**, by Gerald M. Weinberg, explores change management, from systems thinking to project management to technology transfer to the interaction of culture and process. A powerful series conclusion.
   *ISBN: 0-932633-32-3 ©1997 504 pages hardcover*

✔ **Rethinking Systems Analysis & Design**, by Gerald M. Weinberg: Using a short, highly readable essay format, this book presents readers with both the logical and the more intuitive aspects of the analysis/design process.
   *ISBN: 0-932633-08-0 ©1988 208 pages softcover*

✔ **Roundtable on Project Management: A SHAPE Forum Dialogue**, edited by James Bullock, Gerald M. Weinberg, and Marie Benesh: Forty software consultants and managers pool their years of experience and lessons learned from managing software projects. Presented as a fast-paced dialogue, the text captures the most provocative points of debate from Jerry Weinberg's Web-based discussion forum, SHAPE: Software as a Human Activity Performed Effectively.
   *ISBN: 0-932633-48-X ©2001 200 pp. softcover*

✔ **The Secrets of Consulting**, by Gerald M. Weinberg: Shows you how to keep ahead of your clients, create a special "consultant's survival kit," negotiate in difficult situations, measure your effectiveness, market yourself, be yourself, and much more!
   *ISBN: 0-932633-01-3 ©1985 248 pages softcover*

DORSET HOUSE PUBLISHING 353 WEST 12TH STREET NEW YORK, NEW YORK 10014 USA
(800) 342-6657 • (212) 620-4053 • fax (212) 727-1044 • info@dorsethouse.com • www.dorsethouse.com

# DH *More Praise for* <u>The Secrets of Consulting</u>

"If you want to know what makes a consultant work, either because you want to use one or be one, then this is the book you must read. By seeing the view from both sides of the fence, you can plot a successful strategy, independent of whether you are the giver or receiver of the advice."
—CHARLES ASHBACHER
CHARLES ASHBACHER TECHNOLOGIES
POSTED ON AMAZON.COM

"exciting and provocative, bringing fresh insights and perspectives." —*CONSULTANTS NEWS*

"It really does contain those little secrets . . . should make you far more effective for your clients, and far more comfortable with yourself."
—*MICRO CORNUCOPIA*

". . . an irreverent, funny, provocative, satirical but true look at those thousands of professionals, as well as con men, who call themselves consultants." —MARTIN A. GOETZ, PRESIDENT, APPLIED DATA RESEARCH, INC.

"There is much of value in this book for the system professional . . . and highly practical help to anyone who must advise others."
—*JOURNAL OF SYSTEMS MANAGEMENT*

"Weinberg's wisest work! . . . This book is a Sermon on the Mount but more entertaining. Fun airplane reading for all consultants!"
—JAMES MARTIN, NOTED AUTHOR AND LECTURER

"educative, entertaining, and thought-provoking." —*ICCA's THE INDEPENDENT*

". . . entertaining prose littered with humorous paradoxes, dilemmas and contradictions to share his ideas on how to deal with people and organizations to help them change. This book is full of ideas on how to work with people to get them to adopt new ideas." —MARY SAKRY, THE PROCESS GROUP

". . . much more than about giving advice successfully. It's a guide that recognizes and respects the individuality and freedom of each person you deal with in business and social dealings. It's clear-eyed and clever and fun to read. Highly recommended." —HARRY BROWNE
FROM *HOW I FOUND FREEDOM IN AN UNFREE WORLD*

## THE SECRETS OF CONSULTING
BY GERALD M. WEINBERG   FOREWORD BY VIRGINIA SATIR
ISBN: 0-932633-01-3   ©1985   248 PAGES, SOFTCOVER

DORSET HOUSE PUBLISHING  353 WEST 12TH STREET  NEW YORK, NEW YORK 10014 USA
(800) 342-6657 • (212) 620-4053 • fax (212) 727-1044 • info@dorsethouse.com • www.dorsethouse.com